Especially for

....

From

....

Date

....

3-MINUTE
DEVOTIONS

FOR A
Dog Lover's Heart

180 **Paws-itively Perfect** Readings

BARBOUR BOOKS
An Imprint of Barbour Publishing, Inc.

© 2016 by Barbour Publishing, Inc.

Print ISBN 978-1-63409-776-5

eBook Editions:
Adobe Digital Edition (.epub) 978-1-63409-878-6
Kindle and MobiPocket Edition (.prc) 978-1-63409-879-3

Published by Barbour Books, an imprint of Barbour Publishing, Inc., P.O. Box 719, Uhrichsville, Ohio 44683, www.barbourbooks.com

Our mission is to publish and distribute inspirational products offering exceptional value and biblical encouragement to the masses.

Member of the
Evangelical Christian
Publishers Association

Printed in the United States of America.

Introduction

Welcome to *3-Minute Devotions for a Dog Lover's Heart*—a book just for dog lovers! Here you'll find 180 devotional readings celebrating faith, fun, and furry canines, as well as God's love, voice, security, strength, friendship—and more! Ideal for pooch enthusiasts of all ages, these devotions promise bountiful blessings. It's a perfect way to start or end a day, or for a quick pick-me-up in between, all the while helping you grow closer to God and experiencing His joy through the antics of our furry friends!

Call the Expert

*Call to me and I will answer you and tell you great
and unsearchable things you do not know.*
JEREMIAH 33:3 NIV

A show on the National Geographic Channel featured a couple who walked their highly aggressive Great Dane every day to unleash his energy. Unusually aggravated by visitors, he attacked some guests at their home.

The owner jogged him two miles a day and tried to work with him to no avail. Finally, they called a dog expert. Besides the fear driving their pet's unusual aggression, he discovered that the pup needed to unload extra energy. He patiently taught him to swim in their pool, to release his adrenaline into the water—now a canine therapy pool.

Similarly, computer-savvy friends noticed their son was becoming increasingly ill-tempered. They discovered he was texting friends and surfing the Internet into the wee hours of the night. Time limits and history checks hadn't curtailed the clever young student, who navigated filters and even reactivated a dead phone.

As a last resort, they called a local Internet expert who configured two routers: one for their home, the other for their son's computer. Now they could sleep in peace.

Sometimes we try hard on our own to solve difficult problems until we're flustered and tense—when all along God is just waiting for us to call on Him. Do you have a baffling situation? Don't wait to call on the Lord.

**Lord, help me to call on You sooner rather than later.
I know You will lead me to the right solution.**

Through the Storms

*"You have been a refuge for the poor, a refuge
for the needy in their distress, a shelter from
the storm and a shade from the heat."*

ISAIAH 25:4 NIV

Shamgar, our 12-pound Lhasa apso, was named for the biblical
Shamgar. He was one of the twelve judges of Israel, and we know he
killed six thousand Philistines with an ox goad. He saved Israel.

Our Shamgar wasn't quite as brave. Oh, he was a tough talker
when another dog appeared on the other side of a fence or window,
but when the opponent came near, Shamgar would tuck tail and
run. And when a thunderstorm came, he changed from a dog to a
chicken.

At the first thunderclap Shamgar would find me, wherever
I was. If I was sitting down, he'd tuck himself under my arm and
shiver until the storm passed. And if the storm happened at night,
too bad. He'd jump up on the bed and crawl under the covers,
getting as close to me as he could.

As cute and pitiful as that may seem, I can learn a lesson from
Shamgar. Too many times I try to brave life's storms alone. Why
do I do that? I have a Master who loves me and longs to shelter
me. When thunder roars and lightning strikes, I need to tuck
myself under His arm and let Him hold me. The storms may not be
pleasant, but as long as I stay close to the Master, I know He'll see
me through.

Dear Father, Thank You for seeing me through the storms.

The Nugget Bandit

Let your moderation be known unto all men.
PHILIPPIANS 4:5 KJV

When Brianna came home from her job at the hospital, she found her husband asleep on the couch. Assorted fast-food leftovers were on and around him. On his chest rested an empty, large container of chicken nuggets. Half-eaten French fries and a partial beverage sat on the coffee table. James began to stir as Brianna let the dogs out. Their dachshund waddled sluggishly to the door.

That's odd, thought Brianna. *Chuy looks as round as a Christmas turkey.* She shrugged and yawned. It had been a long shift and she was ready to wake James so they could go to bed for the remainder of the night.

"Where are my nuggets?" James mumbled. "Did you eat them?"

Brianna rolled her eyes. "I'm a vegetarian, remember? I have no idea. . .uh oh." Chuy's fat stomach and the by now well-fertilized backyard told the rest of the story.

To overindulge any appetite—whether you're a human or a dog—can bring misery and mess. After Solomon warns of gluttony in the book of Proverbs, he says, "Labour not to be rich" (Proverbs 23:4 KJV). To keep our appetites in check keeps us from extremes in all areas of life. God's cure rests in learning contentment.

Lord Jesus, I pray for balance in my life today in all my pursuits. Help me to be content in You and with what I have.

Your Protector

We know that whoever is born of God does not sin;
but he who has been born of God keeps himself,
and the wicked one does not touch him.

1 JOHN 5:18 NKJV

One afternoon as I got off the school bus at my grandparents'
house, my eyes were drawn to a beautiful German shepherd on a
cable run in the front yard. Grandpa told us to be cautious. "It's
going to take a while for him to know he belongs here. He doesn't
know we are his people just yet," he said. Grandpa introduced us to
Mike, and he took to all of us kids right away.

One winter afternoon, we were outside playing when my
mom opened the gate and drove into the yard. My youngest sister,
Jill, took off running across the yard toward Mom. Mike knew we
weren't supposed to cross the driveway when cars were coming into
the yard. He bolted toward my sister, locked his jaw down on the
hood of her furry pink coat, and held her fast. She kicked, screamed,
and pulled to get away, but he held fast. He was not about to let one
of us near that dangerous car.

As children of God, we belong to our Father. Jesus stands
ready to protect and defend us. Just imagine Him positioning
Himself between you and the devil as you stand in faith.

Father, thank You for sending Your Son to save me.
I trust Him to protect and keep me in all my ways!

To Be Like Frank

Therefore if there is any consolation in Christ, if any comfort of love, if any fellowship of the Spirit, if any affection and mercy, fulfill my joy by being like-minded, having the same love, being of one accord, of one mind.

PHILIPPIANS 2:1–2 NKJV

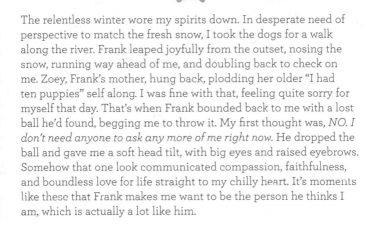

The relentless winter wore my spirits down. In desperate need of perspective to match the fresh snow, I took the dogs for a walk along the river. Frank leaped joyfully from the outset, nosing the snow, running way ahead of me, and doubling back to check on me. Zoey, Frank's mother, hung back, plodding her older "I had ten puppies" self along. I was fine with that, feeling quite sorry for myself that day. That's when Frank bounded back to me with a lost ball he'd found, begging me to throw it. My first thought was, *NO. I don't need anyone to ask any more of me right now.* He dropped the ball and gave me a soft head tilt, with big eyes and raised eyebrows. Somehow that one look communicated compassion, faithfulness, and boundless love for life straight to my chilly heart. It's moments like these that Frank makes me want to be the person he thinks I am, which is actually a lot like him.

Father God, thank You for the beautiful encouragement of Your creation, today, from my dog.

The Dark Tornado

*It's wise to be patient and show
what you are like by forgiving others.*
Proverbs 19:11 CEV

Twister was capable of destroying anything with little more than a mischievous glance and a rapid-fire twisting of his agile body. He destroyed the yard when he was outside. When he was inside, he destroyed anything that couldn't get out of his way. Twister was a force to be reckoned with.

He was a black Lab with an enthusiasm for life that paralleled a child on Christmas morning. He wore a perpetual smirk. His head would rise, his tail would wag, and his body and legs could not stay still. He loved me, but he broke my stuff.

Twister couldn't ask for forgiveness, but he needed it. He couldn't say he was sorry, and I'm not sure he was. Somehow, in spite of his actions, I loved that dog. I am *like* that dog.

Even when I want to do the right thing, I'm almost certain to mess things up. All my trying can result in failure. I need forgiveness, and God gives it to me.

Dear God, forgive me and then help me believe the forgiveness You offer is more than a onetime gift. Help me learn that through Your forgiveness I can grow and thrive. When that happens, help me to say thank You by obeying the Forgiver.

Sweet Aroma

*And walk in love, as Christ also has loved us and given
Himself for us, an offering and a sacrifice to
God for a sweet-smelling aroma.*

EPHESIANS 5:2 NKJV

Tommy is a curious, friendly pup, which would be fine if he used some discernment. He shouldn't investigate everything he finds. Such as skunks.

Our son and his family live in an urban area where residents don't expect wildlife, but for some reason they have an abundance of uninvited guests. Beavers gnaw on their trees, deer leap in front of cars, and skunks reside under the porches. Tommy likes to visit these cute little black and white neighbors and expects them to be friendly. Which creates a problem.

Tommy has long curly hair and short legs—not a good combination when he meets a skunk. Those legs slow his escape and the hair is a nightmare to clean and freshen. Did I mention he isn't a quick learner? So far, he's had four close encounters with skunks.

His family learned the formula for the best odor eradicator, but his forays into the skunk world always happened late at night, right at bedtime. Our son and his wife finally refused to let Tommy in the backyard by himself after dark. He has to be on a leash, while they carry a flashlight and absolutely forbid any friendly visits.

**Heavenly Father, help me be content only to go where
You want me, enjoying the sweet aroma of Your sacrifice.**

Mourn with Those Who Mourn

Rejoice with those who rejoice;
mourn with those who mourn.
ROMANS 12:15 NIV

When I was growing up, my family had a border collie who was very aware of and sensitive to human emotions. Whenever something was upsetting me and I'd sneak away to my room for a good cry, he was usually the first one on the scene to check in on me. He'd walk in quietly, lay his head on my lap, and look up at me with his big brown eyes. He would stay there, sitting quietly next to me, until I felt better. His simple presence was overwhelmingly comforting.

Instead of running away from a potentially awkward situation, embrace the opportunity to be a comfort and support to someone who is hurting. Look out for those who might need an extra hug, smile, or encouraging word. Even if you don't know what to say, just being an empathetic and supporting presence is all that's necessary.

Physical and emotional pain tend to make us feel very alone, so the simple act of noticing that someone is hurting, being there for them, mourning with them, and standing by until they feel better has remarkable power to heal wounds and banish loneliness.

Lord, You are the great Comforter. I pray that You would give me Your eyes to notice those around me who are hurting. I pray that You would use me as Your arms to reach out to them.

True Freedom

*Paul, a servant of God and an apostle of Jesus Christ
to further the faith of God's elect and their
knowledge of the truth that
leads to godliness.*
TITUS 1:1 NIV

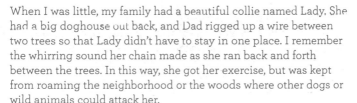

When I was little, my family had a beautiful collie named Lady. She had a big doghouse out back, and Dad rigged up a wire between two trees so that Lady didn't have to stay in one place. I remember the whirring sound her chain made as she ran back and forth between the trees. In this way, she got her exercise, but was kept from roaming the neighborhood or the woods where other dogs or wild animals could attack her.

Consider our restrictions. If we didn't have traffic laws, we'd be overrun with accidents. If we didn't feel pain, we would hurt ourselves without even knowing it. If we could transport ourselves anywhere we wanted by the blink of an eye, would we really stick around and take care of our responsibilities? Healthy restrictions are necessary.

Paul described himself as a bondservant. He put on the chains of servitude to Christ, meaning he voluntarily yielded his life to Jesus. He traveled all over the world in God's will and care, just like Lady was free to roam back and forth, while staying in my family's protection. Being a servant of Christ provides freedom to live a godly life.

**Thank You, God, that obeying You benefits me and my family.
May Your perfect will be done in my life.**

Learning the Way

Show me your ways, Lᴏʀᴅ, teach me your paths.
Guide me in your truth and teach me, for you are God
my Savior, and my hope is in you all day long.

PSALM 25:4–5 NIV

Shortly after Paul's Great Pyrenees died, he adopted Maggie. His
rescued pet could have napped in the bigger dog's water bowl.
Maggie refused to eat for the first few days of her new life with
Paul. He tried every type of dog food he could think of, but nothing
worked. Paul feared for Maggie's life. But then he remembered the
way his Great Pyrenees had devoured cheese even when it wouldn't
touch dog food. Paul tried this trick with Maggie, and soon the
puppy was eating like a champion.

Just as Maggie's owner did the things necessary to ensure
that she grew and thrived, our Savior offers us His way. David's
experiences were limited. When Jesus came, He brought life to
God's way with parables and miracles. His lifestyle taught a great
deal. Jesus showed calmness in handling confrontations. He taught
compassion for people. He modeled how to forgive and how to give
of himself.

It is through the Bible that we discover God's timeless path of
light, enlightenment, and life.

Lord, I accept that You care and love me enough
to teach me Your ways. I am willing to learn.

Space for Everybody

"How good and pleasant it is when God's
people live together in unity!"
PSALM 133:1 NIV

We have three dogs, one cat, and eight pet beds. Currently, all three dogs and the cat are asleep on one cushion. I just peeked into the living room and saw Jot stretching her back legs, which made Tilly scoot to the center of the bed and Black Purrl extend a sleepy paw over Friskie's head. They seem very comfortable in their little nest, cuddled together in drowsy warmth.

The picture isn't always so peaceful. When the kitten first arrived, Tilly thought she was a sort of exotic snack food. Friskie is a relative newcomer and wasn't welcomed to the communal snooze until she picked up on the mood of the older dogs and learned to respect their space. Occasionally there has been territorial sniping when one of the foursome decides to commandeer a special cushion for herself. The seven remaining undisputed cushions are seemingly irrelevant at such times. More often, there is an amicable sharing of resources—one cushion at a time.

The church is full of ordinary people with ordinary desires. It is natural to enjoy one's own space. It is just as necessary to find strength and support in community. We have our differences of opinions and personalities, but in the end we pull together.

Dear Lord, thank You for my local congregation.
Help me rejoice in the diversity and unity of Your people.

Bad Behavior

*Search me, God, and know my heart; test me and know
my anxious thoughts. See if there is any offensive
way in me, and lead me in the way everlasting.*

PSALM 139:23–24 NIV

"Benji did it again, Steve!" I yelled from the living room. "He found a new place."

My husband's voice peaked to a new high. "That's why I don't believe in dogs living in the house—he thinks it's his bathroom."

"But it's not his fault. My other dogs had accidents on the carpet and the old odors fool him."

I can make excuses for Benji, but the truth is, he does what he wants. If it's raining, we let him out. He comes in and we find a new puddle in a different place. He doesn't want to get in trouble. It's his way of cheating.

Truth is, we all have ways to hide and avoid suspicion. We tell our spouse we are going to fill up the car, but a trip to the gas station includes a drive by the donut shop. Work policy states we are not to use the Internet to shop or access personal e-mails during business hours, but how can it hurt one time or two when work is slow?

Schnauzers are stubborn. They do what they want if they can—they're a lot like us. Trouble is, we might be able to hide the truth from others, but we can't hide from God.

**Forgive me, God, for not owning my bad behavior.
Help me to change.**

Hope

*"May your unfailing love be with us, LORD,
even as we put our hope in you."*
PSALM 33:22 NIV

My dog Shamgar thinks more highly of me than he should. He thinks I'm good, kind, and generous. On a good day, I try to be all those things, but not every day is a good day.

One Saturday morning I went into the living room, ready to enjoy my nice, steaming plate of eggs while watching *Looney Tunes*. That's when Shamgar decided to come sit at my feet. It would have been fine if he'd just watched cartoons with me, but no. He sat straight and tall, looking at my eggs and licking his chops. Every once in a while, he'd gaze directly in my eyes with a look of total trust and expectancy.

Now, that's hope.

Before I knew it, I held out a nice-sized chunk of egg for him. He wagged his tail, took the egg, and lay at my feet. He was satisfied. He'd placed his faith in me, and I'd delivered.

I wonder why I don't always have that kind of faith in God. After all, He is good. He is only good, never selfish or self-centered like I am.

Like Shamgar, I need to put my faith and hope in my Master, knowing He loves me with all His heart. I need to sit at His feet and just wait; just trust. My hope in Him will never, ever leave me disappointed.

**Dear Father, thank You for Your constant goodness.
Remind me that nothing is hopeless when I trust in You.**

First, You Gotta Get by Me

If you are determined to go to Egypt and you do go to settle there,
then the sword you fear will overtake you . . . and there you will die.
JEREMIAH 42:15–16 NIV

Larry and his sister Amanda had an ally in the family Doberman, Max. Like most Dobermans, Max could be counted on for his protection and loyalty—even when he lacked discernment.

The two children and their parents learned quickly that spankings would have to be delayed if Max was in the house when Larry or Amanda misbehaved. As deserved as a swat on the fanny might be for one of the siblings, Max would come after the disciplining parent with a police dog's zeal. Since Max's bite was worse than his bark, he had to be put outside before punishment was metered out.

Disobeying God brings correction. Putting ourselves in harm's way with bad decisions or foolish actions leads to consequences. When the Israelites persisted in going their own way, the Lord warned them: *I'll give no protection for disobedience.* Obedience brings favor and protection; disobedience, wrath and protection's absence.

Unlike Max, God feels no obligation to protect us when we blatantly disobey Him. He may show mercy, but we can't assume that will happen. Hopefully, His lack of intervention will teach us wisdom for future choices.

Lord, forgive my willfulness and choices to do things my way.
I want to seek You first and live before You in a pleasing way.

Highly Favored

*For the L*ORD *God is a sun and shield; the L*ORD *bestows favor
and honor; no good thing does he withhold from
those whose walk is blameless.*

PSALM 84:11 NIV

Romeo looks like an Ewok from the *Star Wars* movies. He's half shih
tzu, half dachshund. He quickly chose my husband, Blaine, as his
favorite. Although I know he loves me, if Blaine is home, it's difficult
to separate the two.

About an hour before it's time for Blaine to get home from
work, Romeo perches on the arm of the couch, where he can see out
the window. The instant he hears the garage door open, he darts to
the laundry room and waits for Blaine to come into the house.

Romeo can hardly contain his excitement. He jumps up and
down trying to get Blaine's attention. He can't wait for Blaine to put
his briefcase down and sit down in the floor with him so Romeo can
have his full attention.

Imagine having a relationship like that with God. He loves you
and wants to spend every moment with you. He waits and watches
for you to arrive in His presence. He wants to hear you call His
name and spend time with Him.

**Heavenly Father, thank You for loving me. Thank You for
pouring out Your favor on my life and loving me just as I am.**

She Doesn't Have a Chance

Let us hold tightly without wavering to the hope we affirm,
for God can be trusted to keep his promise. Let us think of ways
to motivate one another to acts of love and good works.

HEBREWS 10:23–24 NLT

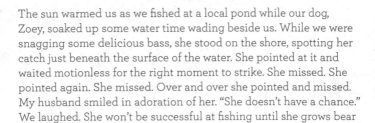

The sun warmed us as we fished at a local pond while our dog, Zoey, soaked up some water time wading beside us. While we were snagging some delicious bass, she stood on the shore, spotting her catch just beneath the surface of the water. She pointed at it and waited motionless for the right moment to strike. She missed. She pointed again. She missed. Over and over she pointed and missed. My husband smiled in adoration of her. "She doesn't have a chance." We laughed. She won't be successful at fishing until she grows bear claws, but she keeps trying and she doesn't seem to lose hope.

Her perseverance teaches me in beautiful ways. In this life, in this fallen state, I cannot expect to have the great claws I wish I had to fully accomplish what I hope to do. But I will one day. For now, God gives me all that I need.

Lord, thank You for the rich truths You show me through Your marvelous works. Strengthen me to keep walking in faith. Amen.

Easter Celebration

This is a day to remember. Each year, from generation to generation, you must celebrate it as a special festival to the LORD.
EXODUS 12:14 NLT

The house was ready for our family to celebrate Easter with dinner together after church. We dyed eggs the day before so our grandchildren could hunt and fill their baskets. The meal would be ready soon after everyone arrived.

Typical of Kansas, the day turned cold and rainy. Hiding eggs outside couldn't happen, so we tucked them here and there throughout the house before we left home that morning.

It didn't occur to us that Mickey, our little poodle-mix, might think all those eggs were special treats for her. When we returned, we knew immediately we had a problem. From the front door we could see several piles of chewed-up eggs, complete with colored shells, dotting the carpet. Mickey cowered under the desk. Beneath her dark curly hair, she was probably a little green.

While I hurried to clean up the mess, my husband, Jerry, called a 24-hour vet to see if it could have really hurt her. When we learned she'd just have to get it out of her system, my sympathy toward her evaporated. Fortunately, the family began to arrive, so Mickey didn't discover how frustrated I was. The story gave us plenty of laughs, which tempered my temper.

Dear Lord, teach me to celebrate the joy of Your resurrection without concern for insignificant things that can distract me from what is truly important.

In Your Presence

Better is one day in your courts than a thousand elsewhere;
I would rather be a doorkeeper in the house of my
God than dwell in the tents of the wicked.

PSALM 84:10 NIV

One of the dogs that my husband and I fostered absolutely loved going to my in-laws' farm, where he could roam around off leash. The farm is, of course, full of fascinating smells and acres of land to explore. We'd often just sit on the front porch and let him have the run of the farm. Within two or three minutes of exploring he would always come back and sit down next to us or lie down at our feet. There was a plethora of places to explore, animals to chase, and things to smell, yet his greatest desire was to be with us. He would turn down a virtual doggie-paradise in order to sit in our presence.

How much do you desire God's presence? Would you give up the pleasures and enticements of this world just for the opportunity to be with Him? Does your time with Him and in His Word take priority in your life?

The psalmist David understood that in God's presence is fullness of joy (Psalm 16:11). If you notice a lack of joy in your life, maybe you need to stop exploring the things of this world and instead go to your Father, be still (Psalm 46:10), rest in Him, and discover the fulfillment that can only be found when walking with your Father.

Father, keep me from being distracted from the things
of this world. Grant me a consuming desire to
be with You and to know You better.

Persistence

And will not God bring about justice for his chosen ones,
who cry out to him day and night?
LUKE 18:7 NIV

In our country neighborhood, my neighbors, cousins, sisters, and
I would play together daily: house, spaceship, and acting out TV
shows. One day we noticed a thin black dog with brown eyebrows
following us around. We all decided to name her. She wasn't quite a
dog, too old to be a puppy. Pog didn't sound right, so we called her
Duppy.

Upon further inquiry, we found out a neighbor had rescued
the dog, telling the previous owner that one of the kids in the
neighborhood would probably want her. Duppy would follow us
around and try to sneak in an open door. My sister and I would let
Duppy in, despite my parents' protests. One time at supper, when I
saw Dad sneaking Duppy a bite of his food, I knew we had him.

We got consent from our parents and then from the neighbor
who had rescued her. He said we could have her, since that was
his plan all along. Duppy was persistent about finding a home. My
sister and I were persistent about adopting her. Sometimes we do
not receive from the Lord because we give up. Remember Jesus'
parable of the persistent widow (Luke 18:1–8). Keep praying for
those people and issues God puts on your heart.

Lord, increase my faith, so that I will not give up
on receiving the answers to my prayers.

Stinky Stuff

A person may think their own ways are right,
but the LORD weighs the heart.
PROVERBS 21:2 NIV

"Benji, what's that stinky stuff?" I stooped down and inhaled. "Whew!"

I toted Benji to the tub and sat on the edge. I used the nozzle attachment to spray the little stinker down. Benji planted his forepaws on the tub ledge, preparing for a quick escape. I washed as much as possible in this position.

"Nope, Benji, your forepaws, too. . .can't wash some and not all." I forced his forelegs down to the tub bottom. Dirty water streamed from his little legs toward the drain. Disgruntled, he stared at me coldly.

"It's either all clean or all dirty." I stood my ground.

Sometimes we have the misconception that what we do is only our business, especially if it doesn't seem to affect anyone else. It takes time and energy for caring people to help us or even confront our issues. Although it is for our own good, we often resent their attempts.

God often urges us to be "all in" and give our best effort. We want to get by with a halfhearted apology or only do some of our chores or work responsibilities—but we soon find that our half-hearted attempts do not suffice.

Are we in need of attitude adjustments and fresh starts?

Lord, clean my heart and help me to be the best I can be.

Warrior

"Ah, Sovereign LORD, you have made the heavens and the earth
by your great power and outstretched arm.
Nothing is too hard for you."

JEREMIAH 32:17 NIV

Ginger is three months old and weighs less than ten pounds.
Yesterday, she dragged my son's archery target—which is more than
twice her size—around the yard as if she were David and the target
was Goliath. If I hadn't taken it away from her, it would have been in
pieces all over the lawn.

I love that she wasn't intimidated by the size of the thing.
She sees herself not as a tiny pup, but as a fierce warrior. She had
full confidence that, given the chance, she could obliterate that
oversized foam enemy.

We often view the trials we are facing as enormous, while
seeing ourselves as small and weak. Why do we forget that the God
of the universe lives inside us? There is no mountain too tall, no
storm too fierce for God. With Him on our side, we can face any
hardship with confidence that we will win. Like Ginger, we need to
believe we are warriors, not weaklings.

Dear Father, thank You for the reminder that nothing is too hard
for You. Help me to see myself not as a lone, weak victim,
but as a warrior who is already on the winning team.

Retired

*Work willingly at whatever you do, as though you were
working for the Lord rather than for people.*
COLOSSIANS 3:23 NLT

The Chihuahua in the Taco Bell commercials of the mid-1990s
struck a chord with my late father-in-law. That Chihuahua, Gidget,
made him grin every time her small face with those big eyes
appeared on the television screen. Dad had toy Gidgets all over the
house and in the rear window of his car.

In the book *Animal Stars* (New World Library, 2014), trainer
Sue Chipperton said that Gidget never had to perform any tricks in
the commercials, but she was still one hardworking dog. After her
stint in the Taco Bell commercials, Gidget got few acting jobs. She
was forced into retirement, but Sue loved her and kept her as her
own long after the fame and fortune disappeared.

A dear pastor friend once told us before he retired, "What I *do*
is so much a part of who I *am* that I'm not sure I'll like retirement."
But whether we're working, unemployed, or retired, the Bible gives
one instruction for all of life. "Whatever you do or say, do it as a
representative of the Lord Jesus" (Colossians 3:17 NLT).

Lord, no matter what, I want to honor You throughout my life.

The Comforter

"Comfort, comfort my people," says your God. "Speak tenderly to Jerusalem. Tell her that her sad days are gone and her sins are pardoned."

ISAIAH 40:1–2 NLT

Romeo, our half shih tzu, half dachshund, loves to burrow between the sheets in our bed in the early morning. I wondered at first if he was cold. Then I realized it's just natural for his dachshund side to burrow. They like to snuggle down under the weight of a light blanket. It's comforting to them.

Early in the morning I feel him move from the foot of the bed. He brings his sweet little face close to mine as if to ask, "You want to snuggle?" I lift the covers and he wiggles his way about halfway down and rests his back against me.

Our heavenly Father is a great comfort. Sometimes we need to burrow down into His presence and rest there, letting His great love cover us and fill us.

Father, thank You for comforting me when things don't go the way I'd like them to go. I draw strength today as I rest in Your presence.

Down Disaster

My brethren, count it all joy when you fall into various trials,
knowing that the testing of your faith produces patience.
But let patience have its perfect work, that you may
be perfect and complete, lacking nothing.

JAMES 1:2–4 NKJV

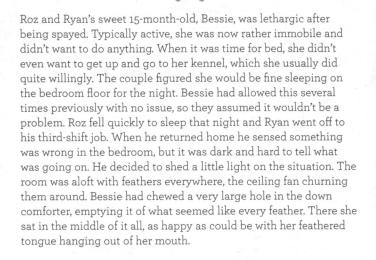

Roz and Ryan's sweet 15-month-old, Bessie, was lethargic after
being spayed. Typically active, she was now rather immobile and
didn't want to do anything. When it was time for bed, she didn't
even want to get up and go to her kennel, which she usually did
quite willingly. The couple figured she would be fine sleeping on
the bedroom floor for the night. Bessie had allowed this several
times previously with no issue, so they assumed it wouldn't be a
problem. Roz fell quickly to sleep that night and Ryan went off to
his third-shift job. When he returned home he sensed something
was wrong in the bedroom, but it was dark and hard to tell what
was going on. He decided to shed a little light on the situation. The
room was aloft with feathers everywhere, the ceiling fan churning
them around. Bessie had chewed a very large hole in the down
comforter, emptying it of what seemed like every feather. There she
sat in the middle of it all, as happy as could be with her feathered
tongue hanging out of her mouth.

**God, thank You for the good that You somehow forge from
the crazy circumstances of life. I am thankful that I
can trust You in whatever frenzy I find myself.**

Beethoven's Snooze

He who has ears to hear, let him hear!
MATTHEW 11:15 NKJV

I'd just moved into my first home. Young and on my own, I needed a dog. His name was Beethoven, a hound dog that slept where he wanted, ate whatever he could find, and disregarded every command.

I came home from work one day to find he'd used an electrical cord as a chew toy, ate a hole in an heirloom quilt, and had the audacity to fall asleep in the middle of the incriminating evidence, snoring like a freight train. This followed a trail of similar behavior.

I gave him a piece of my mind. I held up the evidence. I pleaded for a change in behavior. Still he snored and ignored.

When I touched his back he suddenly became highly motivated. He rose defensively and then greeted me with genuine affection. That was the day I learned Beethoven was deaf. He couldn't respond to my commands because he couldn't hear them. He couldn't understand. He'd never heard my voice.

Hearing gives us opportunity to understand. Hearing gives us new information. Hearing invites friendship.

Even when we can't physically hear, God has given us all we need to understand, *hear*, and obey in the Bible. Read—and hear Him speak.

Dear God, You want me to listen. You want me to understand. Help me read Your words and let them speak to the deepest part of me. Let me hear Your voice and follow Your lead.

Freely Give, Freely Receive

So let each one give as he purposes in his heart,
not grudgingly or of necessity; for God loves a cheerful giver.
2 CORINTHIANS 9:7 NKJV

Our nephew was going on a trip and asked us to watch Jazz, his beagle. Alec offered to reciprocate when we needed a dog-sitter, so it sounded like a good plan. Our dog wasn't used to hosting four-footed guests, but when Jazz arrived, after only a couple of sniffs, Jazz and Mickey accepted each other as friends.

Jazz enjoyed special gourmet food. Mickey ate whatever was on sale when we restocked. The first day, we put their food bowls fairly close together and left them to eat their dinners. There wasn't any commotion, so we figured all was well. Both bowls were empty when we checked.

I was surprised that Mickey didn't go for Jazz's food—it definitely smelled better. A couple days later, when I filled their bowls, I paid more attention. Mickey headed straight for Jazz's food while Jazz sat back, patiently waiting without showing any resistance. I didn't discipline Mickey, because they seemed to have some sort of understanding. After Mickey ate what she wanted, she headed for her own bowl and filled her mouth. Jazz finished his meal while Mickey trotted to a chair in the family room and nuzzled under a cushion. When I checked, there was a stash of Mickey's food.

Heavenly Father, teach me to give joyfully
and never hoard what I have.

Starved

*Like newborn babies, crave pure spiritual milk, so that by
it you may grow up in your salvation, now that you
have tasted that the Lord is good.*

1 PETER 2:2–3 NIV

One of the dogs that I fostered was rescued from a dog-fighting ring where she was kept chained up her entire life with minimal food. When she came into the rescue, she was a heart-wrenchingly pitiful sight with ribs, hip bones, and skull protruding under her sore-covered coat.

Needless to say, she loved food. She would (and certainly tried to) eat anything. When I put food in front of her she would devour it as though it was her last meal. She knew from personal experience that it is painful and unhealthy to go without food.

Unfortunately, we often don't realize how unhealthy it is to starve ourselves of spiritual food. God's Word is our spiritual sustenance, and yet, do you crave it and try to pick it up wherever and whenever you can? Or do you ignore the "hunger pains" of a life devoid of God's Word? Pray that God would give you a ravenous appetite for spiritual bread.

The physical growth of my foster dog had been stunted because of her lack of nutrition, and she certainly would have wasted away had she not been mercifully rescued. In the same way, you will experience no spiritual growth or lifesaving nourishment apart from God's Word and fellowship with Him and other believers. Don't starve yourself of the bountiful feast God has offered you.

**Sustainer of all life, grant me a ravenous appetite for Your Word.
Help me to recognize that I am starving apart from You.
May I be satiated with Your truth.**

My Doggies, Angel Guardians

For he shall give his angels charge over thee,
to keep thee in all thy ways.

PSALM 91:11 KJV

The way my mom and dad tell the story, I was three years old when I decided to take a walk with the two family dogs. Sadie was a gentle German shepherd/collie mix. Bobby was a spunky golden collie. My family lived on a farm in rural Pennsylvania. Dad worked in the city and would come back to the farm on weekends. On that particular day, Mom was busy with chores and thought somebody else in the family was watching me.

Guess I was too fast for them. I slipped out the door without anybody noticing. But my two faithful canine companions noticed and wouldn't let me out of their sight. This was reported by a neighbor couple who were driving down the country road that led past our string of farmhouses. They were surprised to see a little girl walking at the side of the main road.

But I wasn't alone. Two dogs flanked me on both sides. "They wouldn't let that child step out into the road," Mr. Clark told my shocked family after he and his wife retrieved me and the dogs and delivered us back home. Sometimes we walk through life with angels to the left and right of us. It's possible our loving dogs could serve as angels on earth.

Thank You, Lord, for protecting us in all
of our journeys through life.

Return

*"And if I go and prepare a place for you,
I will come back and take you to be with me."*
JOHN 14:3 NIV

Hachi is an amazing movie based on a true story about a dog in Japan who loved his master. A professor discovered the collared Akita Inu pup, "Hachiko," where he daily rode the train to work. Unable to find his owner, Hachi's loyalty won the professor's heart.

The two became inseparable. Like clockwork, each morning Hachi joyfully escorted his master to work and watched him board the train. Every afternoon Hachi faithfully waited at the station for his master's return to accompany him home. The town people, familiar with their routine, contributed to the daily celebration of man and dog by greeting Hachi, feeding him treats, and sharing his affection.

Then, one day the professor died at the university.

Hachi waited to meet him, steadfast through the night. For over a decade, Hachi lived under an abandoned rail car. Each afternoon he returned to the same spot, waiting for the train's arrival. The community cared for him as he continued his routine, always hoping to greet his master.

Some of us have lost loved ones. Like Hachi, we yearn to see them and feel their touch. As we look to the heavens where we will again greet them someday, we also patiently wait and anticipate the return of our heavenly Master.

**Thank You, Lord, for being faithful to Your promises.
We will not be disappointed.**

Staying Clean

Do not let your heart turn to her ways or stray into her paths.
Many are the victims she has brought down;
her slain are a mighty throng.

PROVERBS 7:25–26 NIV

Moses, a fluffy, white-haired Shorkie, looked like the sweetest, most angelic little thing. But looks can be deceiving, and Moses had a devilish side. While most of his pranks and antics were cute, he did something that couldn't be ignored.

He killed one of our chickens.

We disciplined him. We did all we could to keep him away from the chickens. But once he'd experienced the taste of those yummy Kentucky-fried feathers, he wanted more. No matter what we did, Moses was now a chicken addict.

Though it broke our hearts, we realized there was no rehab center for Moses. We found him a new loving home with a big backyard and no chickens. Without temptation clucking in his face, Moses is now clean and sober.

We all struggle with one sin or another. For some, it's alcohol or drugs. For others, it's gossip or gluttony. Sometimes the best thing we can do to resist temptation is to remove ourselves from it. That takes self-discipline, but God will give us the strength to say no, and He will reward our efforts.

Dear Father, help me to stay far away from the things that tempt me to sin. I want to honor You with my choices.

Irritants

After he [Jesus] had dismissed them,
he went up on a mountainside by himself to pray.
MATTHEW 14:23 NIV

Our four young grandsons came for a visit. With animal fur and dander allergies rampant in our family, the boys have not been around pets much. So when Rocket, the cocker spaniel next door, came to investigate the squirt gun battle going on in our backyard, the attack started.

A moving, furry target! The boys took aim, and it was four against one. The "one" had no squirt gun of his own. What should he do? I could almost hear Rocket's thoughts.

Who are these pesky irritants? Should I run away, or go after one and scatter the rest?

Although we may not find other people as irritating as Rocket did that day, we all need time alone. Young moms especially find such times a rare, coveted commodity. The Lord understands this deep-seated need of ours. He made time for privacy and aloneness with His disciples. "Come with me by yourselves to a quiet place and get some rest" (Mark 6:31 NIV).

This grandma stopped the boys-against-unarmed-dog skirmish. If a good friend or relative offers you some respite today from an irritant or heavy responsibility, take it and run! Enjoy it as a blessing from the Lord.

Lord, sometimes I need some quiet time and space
with You. I pray to be humble enough to ask for
it, and to return the favor when needed.

He is with You in Loss

You have turned for me my mourning into dancing; You have put
off my sackcloth and clothed me with gladness, To the end
that my glory may sing praise to You and not be silent.
O LORD my God, I will give thanks to You forever.

PSALM 30:11–12 NKJV

One crisp autumn morning Blaine walked outside to greet his
beautiful white German shepherd, Misty. Surprised not to see her,
he called her name, but received no reply.

His heart sank into his stomach and tears welled in his eyes
as he sensed his companion since childhood might have died. His
eyes fell to her white body bedded down next to the garage door. As
he gently touched her with his foot, he realized she'd been gone for
a while. He remembered the day he got her. Her beautiful blue eyes
had sparkled with joy as he lifted her into his arms. *She was a good*
friend, he thought, *and I'm going to miss her.*

As he dug a hole on the back side of the family's five acres to
lay her to rest, he thanked her for the many loyal years of love and
memories. He thanked God for bringing her into his life.

Father, thank You for the love and devotion from those
I love. When they leave my life, comfort me and give
me strength to open my heart to new friendships.

Black Snow Day

Bessie had just turned a year old on Valentine's Day, and now she and her owner, Roz, were going to get a nice snow day together at home. The school where Roz worked was closed, so she decided to relax in her pajamas for a while and work on some church things that she needed to tend to. She settled in with her laptop, coffee, paperwork, and pens. While Roz worked, Bessie nuzzled in beside her, sleeping so soundly she snored. Roz thought this would be a good time for a quick shower. After her shower she checked on Bessie, who was still asleep, but in a different position. After a while, Bessie got up and whined at the door to go out. Roz noticed a smudge on Bessie's tail as she walked away from the house. When she turned around she noticed the black smudge on the kitchen floor, and black paw prints that led to a black trail through the dining room and behind a chair to the biggest black blob of ink she'd ever seen. Bessie had apparently accomplished all of this during Roz's shower. Bessie stood at the door waiting to be let in with her black tongue hanging out between black lips.

Lord? Lord?! Okay, yes, You are here, I know. In the midst of my trials, thank You for somehow having purpose in it all, even when I don't see it.

Ask and You Will Receive

"Yes it is, Lord," she said. "Even the dogs eat the crumbs that fall from their master's table."

MATTHEW 15:27 NIV

Restaurants in the United States tend to discriminate against man's best friend more than many nations. Several countries we've visited let people bring dogs into restaurants, though they usually must keep the animals on a leash or lap. When we visited Israel, we often ate at outdoor cafes, where patrons' dogs were welcome and neighborhood dogs knew they could find some snacks.

One day a brownish, long-haired dog studied us from a distance with big, soulful eyes. He ignored the people at the other tables, but gradually moved closer and closer to ours. We didn't encourage him, just enjoyed our meal and chuckled about being his target.

He finally made his way right next to our table and watched each bite as it went into our mouths. After a long, patient wait, he gently tapped his paw against my leg, gazing at me as though I was his last hope for survival. He was obviously well-fed, but we couldn't resist his cunning ways. We wondered how he had learned to zero in on one particular diner for each meal. He obviously knew a tender pat on the leg and that pathetic look would get him some tidbits from our plates.

**Dear heavenly Father, You invite us to ask,
and when we do, You give more than mere crumbs.
You feed our souls with Your riches.**

Rescued

For he has rescued us from the dominion of darkness
and brought us into the kingdom of the Son he loves,
in whom we have redemption, the forgiveness of sins.
COLOSSIANS 1:13–14 NIV

It was 3 a.m. on a rainy morning when Minnie was rescued. Her rescuer snuck into the compound where she was kept to cut the heavy chain that held her in place and dragged her emaciated neck to the ground. Later, when recounting the story, Minnie's rescuer told me that she had completely forgotten to bring a leash. After cutting Minnie's chain, she just had to hope that Minnie would follow her back to the car through the downpour.

Minnie did follow, right at her savior's heels. A picture was taken on her freedom ride that captured her starved little face peeking out from a warm blanket with a look of utmost gratefulness in her beautiful brown eyes.

Though you may not have as dramatic a rescue story as Minnie, you must never forget that you were rescued from a dark domain. Your heavy chain was cut and you were set free.

Minnie followed her rescuer because, by setting her free, that woman had proven to Minnie that she could be trusted. Christ stretched out His arms for you on the cross and died for your freedom. Hasn't He proven His love for you? When He asks you to walk through the darkness, He only asks you to walk where He has already been. So keep close to Him, knowing that He can be trusted. He walks ahead of you through the downpour and the veil of tears to secure a place for you in His glorious Kingdom.

Savior, never let me lose sight of You through the darkness. Thank You for being my Rescuer and Redeemer.

Chicken Mush

And we know that in all things God works for the good of those who love him, who have been called according to his purpose.

ROMANS 8:28 NIV

My sisters and I had our dog, Duppy, as our own, but Dad, an avid hunter, valued his hunting dogs, two beagles named Smokey and Sam. They were helpful in "kicking out" game. Though the beagles were mostly Dad's, we loved and cared for them, too.

One day after school, Dad, with a serious face, showed us red, angry welts on his arms. He had gotten stung several times while trying to rescue Sam, who had gotten into a hornets' nest. Dad didn't expect his dog to make it. He had taken him down in the cellar to die, so we wouldn't have to see him.

We were all sad. To make matters worse, with all the commotion, Mom hadn't been keeping an eye on supper and she'd overcooked the chicken. She put it in gravy and served it over toast. None of us liked it. Dad had an idea. He carried Sam up from the cellar and laid him on blankets in the living room. He gave his chicken mush to Sam. To our surprise and delight, Sam licked the plate clean. We gave him all of our leftover chicken mush and Sam got better. Sometimes the Lord uses the messes in our lives for our benefit.

Lord, thank You for turning the bad things in my life to good.

Friendliness is Next to Godliness

*Dear friends, since God so loved us, we also ought to love one
another. No one has ever seen God; but if we love one another,
God lives in us and his love is made complete in us.*

1 JOHN 4:11–12 NIV

The dog race reflected the Humane Society's sense of humor. For
their first-ever mixed-breed dog race, they picked the greyhound
racing track.

When the referee called out medium-sized dogs, Barney led
his long-eared Basset puppy, Waldo, to the start line. With admirers
stroking his shiny fur, he was in no hurry to get there.

"Owners, take your places at the finish line!"

The start whistle tweeted. Owners shouted for their dogs. All
canines ran to the finish—except one. Waldo ambled toward Barney
for twenty feet then veered into the crowd. Waldo never made it to
the finish line.

"Too friendly," Barney complained when he found his pet.

In the big picture, friendliness is next to godliness. It's a get-
in-your-face kind of love. It shows people that they matter and you
have time for them. Waldo had the right idea. His first choice was
making time for others.

Sharing time, listening, and being friendly are genuine ways
to break down walls and show love outside of your usual circles of
friends and family. How can you make your circle bigger?

**Dear God, give me new opportunities to be
friendly and show care to others.**

43

Dogs of the Titanic

*Out of the depths I cry to you, L*ORD*; Lord, hear my voice.*
Let your ears be attentive to my cry for mercy.

PSALM 130:1–2 NIV

The passenger liner RMS *Titanic* collided with an iceberg twenty minutes before midnight on April 14, 1912. The vessel broke in two from the weight of water it was taking on and sank to the bottom of the cold North Atlantic two hours and forty minutes later, at 2:20 a.m. on April 15, 1912 (ship's time). As people of faith, we know that the Lord is with us in good times and bad. I've always been inspired by the stories of courage and selfless heroism displayed by ordinary people caught up in the turmoil of that extraordinary night.

There were 705 human survivors. Human deaths were approximately 1,514. There were animal survivors, too. Twelve dogs were known to be kept in kennels on F deck. Three survived the sinking. Those three small dogs were carried by their owners (smuggled, really) into lifeboats, tucked inside coats. In one known case, a larger dog was denied entry to a lifeboat and left behind. Margaret Hays carried her Pomeranian, Lady, into lifeboat 7. Elizabeth Rothschild and her Pomeranian found refuge in lifeboat 6. Mr. and Mrs. Henry Hays brought their Pekingese, Sun Yat-Sen, into lifeboat 3. The animals were so small they could be easily concealed under coats or bundled like infants, which enabled them to survive.

Lord, we bow our heads in prayer as we
remember that all life is sacred.

Our Daily Mouse

Do not forget to do good and to share with others,
for with such sacrifices God is pleased.
HEBREWS 13:16 NIV

Midge was the result of a late-night visit to our family pet Minnie by a rogue terrier with dubious intentions. The result was one part English bulldog, one part terrier, and one part cat.

Let me explain.

Her body and coloring bore a striking resemblance to her bulldog mom. Her head was all terrier. She spent most of her life with my grandma, Esther. Midge would waddle from the back door to the chicken coop, which is where she demonstrated the skill of a cat. Midge's favorite gifts were the remnants of mice found while harassing the chickens. Perhaps she believed bad company corrupts good chickens.

For years Midge would haul dozens of mice to the doorstep of her beloved Esther. Each day my grandmother removed the detestable rodents while detailing the reasons the daily deposit was not necessary. Midge just smiled.

What would happen if we had the same dedication to God that Midge had to my grandmother? What if we actually paid attention to His commands and followed them as faithfully? Would it change us? Would it change the world?

Dear God, You want me to be dedicated to You. You want me to learn Your plan, commit to Your plan, and do what You created me to do. Help me never to take lightly the plans You have for me. In the love You have for me, guide my next step and always walk with me.

45

Mellow Yellow

The one who has knowledge uses words with restraint,
and whoever has understanding is even-tempered.
PROVERBS 17:27 NIV

When I pull into the driveway, Sam, my yellow Lab, leaps from the backseat and heads straight to the water bowl in the garage. Benji, my mini-schnauzer, hops down from his passenger seat and beelines to our Heritage tree on the front lawn, where squirrels scamper on the trunk and branches.

Sam's thirst satisfied, he searches the garage for a tennis ball. Once found, he swoops it up, turns with a tail swish, and saunters happily back to plop down at the garage entrance. The green ball safely clutched in his jaws, Sam scopes out our street and occasionally glances at Benji.

By this time, Benji stands quaking on his back legs, forepaws planted on the base of the ash tree, and staring up the trunk, much to the amusement of the squirrels. As his barks turn to shrieks of frustration from lack of squirrel attention, Sam's head melts down to his paws for a nap.

Benji's barks are as annoying as the sound of an alarm clock early in the morning. Sam hears watchdog Benji at the window often. Sam just seems to know when Benji's rantings are not directed toward him—he just ignores them.

Some of us work or live with people who are a lot like Benji. We could learn a lot from Sam.

Lord, grant me tolerance and understanding
for those who squawk unnecessarily.

Conversation

Pray continually.
1 THESSALONIANS 5:17 NIV

Ginger, our little Basset hound, is best friends with our son, FJ. The two of them love to romp and play fetch and splash in puddles. Every moment with those two is a Norman Rockwell moment. But perhaps the funniest, most entertaining thing they do together is talk.

FJ will start a conversation with her. He looks deep into her eyes as if he's sharing a secret, and he'll talk in a serious tone. Then he'll grow quiet, and she'll hold eye contact and talk back. They'll go on like this for several minutes at a time. Sometimes FJ will burst into song, and she'll join him with her off-pitch howl.

Just as FJ is delighted with these chats with Ginger, God loves it when we converse with Him. Sometimes we forget that prayer is a two-way exchange. We talk, then we listen to Him. Then we talk some more, and listen some more. Sometimes we might even burst into a song of praise.

Talking to God is easy. He doesn't expect lofty language or limited, appropriate topics. He wants us to say what's on our minds.

Listening is done through reading His Word, and through being still and letting His Holy Spirit speak to our hearts. When we take time to dialogue with God in this way, He is delighted, and we gain the peace that comes from a close relationship with our Master.

**Dear Father, I'm glad I can talk to You about anything.
Help me to listen to You, as well.**

Not What We Expected

I sought the LORD, and he answered me.
PSALM 34:4 NIV

For years, Pattie and her husband had prayed for a good man for their daughter. "Bless her with a little romance," they had prayed. "She is so lonely."

Yet pretty, well-educated, and godly Elisa remained single. Then God brought Luci Mae into Elisa's life. Elisa found herself lonely no more with her new four-legged companion. The special man didn't come for some time after Luci's arrival, but Pattie laughs. "You gotta love the process," she says. "Luci Mae has my eyes."

Have you ever had a prayer answered far differently than you expected? You may have prayed for a stress-free job—and then lost your job. Maybe you prayed for God's healing, but instead He brought someone to you who needed your empathetic understanding. Maybe you prayed for a human companion, then found yourself with a doting dog instead.

The apostle Paul had prayed to go to Rome to meet with the church there. God did answer his prayer, but not as Paul had anticipated. Paul went to Rome as a prisoner of the state. (See Romans 1:10 and Acts 28:14–16.)

Struggling with unanswered prayer in your life? Look to see if the answer has come wrapped in some packaging you never anticipated—like a Luci Mae.

Lord, You know the deepest prayers of my heart.
Help me to recognize the answers when they come,
and to wait patiently until they do.

Resurrection Life

Eternal life is to know you, the only true God,
and to know Jesus Christ, the one you sent.
JOHN 17:3 CEV

Our gentle German shepherd, Simon, would eat anything—
tomatoes, green beans, and even peaches. Simon's eating habits
never occurred to my parents, aunts, and uncles as they hid Easter
eggs for my sisters, cousins, and me to find one Easter Sunday when
I was a preteen.

No matter how hard we searched, our baskets only contained
plastic eggs. None of the hard-boiled eggs we'd colored were found.
My mother and aunt kept asking, "Did you look here?" Finally, my
dad saw Simon come around from the back of the house with a little
evidence on his face. Dad surmised Simon had swallowed the boiled
Easter eggs whole—shells and all.

Like the colorful Easter eggs Simon swallowed, the power of
death is swallowed up in the victory of Jesus Christ's resurrection.
As joint heirs with Jesus, we have eternal life and death has no
power over us. Death has disappeared into eternal life.

Jesus, thank You for giving Your life for mine.
Through Your death, burial, and resurrection, I can live
for all eternity. Eternity is now. My life with You begins
today. I don't have to fear death, because I have
a promise to live forever as a child of God.

Wait

My soul, wait silently for God alone, for my expectation
is from Him. He only is my rock and my
salvation; He is my defense.
PSALM 62:5–6 NKJV

Bessie waits for her masters wherever they are. Every time. If one of them is in the bathroom or bedroom, she waits at the door until they come out. If she knows there is about an hour before Dad is going to get home from work, she goes to the front door and she sits and waits for him, expectant and excited for his return. Never once does Bessie whine with impatience. She simply waits.

This so beautifully reflects how we ought to wait for the Lord. In our conversations with Him, we need to sit and wait with expectancy. The more the clock ticks, the more excited we should get to hear from Him. This is what He asks of us: to be still in our waiting, and not to be anxious.

Lord, increase my faith today to wait patiently for Your answers. I need to hear from You. Help me to trust that You know exactly the right time.

Husky Angel

Snow fell like fluffy feathers and piled up quickly on our driveway, so I knew I had to shovel. My husband was out of town and it would be dark when the kids got home from school. I bundled up against the icy weather and trudged outside, definitely not excited about the chore. Our drive seemed much longer than usual, with snow growing deeper by the moment.

It was beautiful, but the snow was heavy as I scooped, lifted, and tossed. Before I was halfway finished, I wanted to quit. I leaned on the snow shovel to catch my breath, when something bumped against my leg. My heard thudded. I turned and looked down into the striking blue eyes of a Siberian husky. His look seemed wise, like he understood how tired I felt.

I stooped down, rubbed his fur, and searched for a tag. He was clean, well-fed, and obviously someone's pet. I chatted with him about shoveling snow, and he nudged me as if to say, "You can finish this." As I continued working, he moved along with me. Somehow the snow wasn't as heavy and the wind didn't seem so cold.

When the drive was cleared, I wanted to thank my new friend with a treat, but he had disappeared as silently as he appeared. I never saw him again.

**Lord, You encourage and refresh me
when I'm weary. Thank You!**

51

Peaceful Sleep

In peace I will lie down and sleep,
for you alone, LORD, make me dwell in safety.
PSALM 4:8 NIV

Jackson was abandoned by his family and dropped at a shelter, where he stayed for three months. The day he was scheduled to be euthanized, a rescue organization stepped in and brought him into their program.

After those three months in a remarkably stressful environment—sleeping on a concrete floor in a small enclosure surrounded by unknown dogs—Jackson came home with me as a temporary foster. I bought him a big pillow and a soft blanket to sleep on. Almost immediately after coming home he curled up on that pillow and slept. . .and slept. He was the picture of exhausted, yet peaceful sleep. He knew he was safe. He knew he could finally let his guard down and rest.

Though at times you may find it difficult to sleep through the chaos of this world, remember that you sleep in the shadow of God's wings, where nothing outside of His plan dare touch you. In the security that God alone provides, you can stand unwaveringly courageous in the face of whatever heartaches this life is capable of, knowing that Jesus has overcome the world (John 16:33).

Jackson came close to the end of his story, yet that fateful day proved to actually be the beginning of a much more beautiful chapter for him. In the same way, no matter what happens here on earth, the end of your earthly story is the beginning of a far better eternal life.

Almighty God, grant me the incomprehensible
peace that You alone can offer.

It's All in the Eyes

Dear friends, since God so loved us,
we also ought to love one another.

1 JOHN 4:11 NIV

I bought a quilting kit with a puppy motif and was stitching one of the pieces when my niece dropped by. "How precious," she said. "The puppy on that square looks just like Lady." Lady is our golden retriever, a rescue dog we got from the animal shelter. My husband and I enjoy her love and company so much.

"This pattern reminds me of how Lady looks at me," I said. "I'll look up and see her bright eyes fixed on me and I wonder what she's thinking."

My niece laughed. "She's probably thinking, 'Thanks for taking me home, Mom. I'm glad I ended up with you.'" She checked out the pattern on the box. "Where's the slogan? The quilt should have a slogan, like 'Love is a warm puppy.'"

"I could always add something," I said. "But look at how the squares fit together. All the dogs are looking out at you. Maybe that's the point they're making—that we're the focus of our dogs' world. They give love and depend on us for love."

Dogs can't talk, but it's all in the eyes. They tell you everything with those long, soulful looks. I decided not to stitch any slogans on the quilt. I let the puppies on that quilt talk for themselves.

Lord, help us to love each other with the simple,
honest love that our animal friends have for us.

Strawberry Tops

Be devoted to one another in love.
Honor one another above yourselves.
ROMANS 12:10 NIV

"Shake, Sam!" I dangled a strawberry top before Sam, shook his raised paw, dropped the leafy stem into Sam's jaws and popped the berry into mine. My Lab sat at attention in the kitchen, ready to obey any command for another juicy treat. Benji, my schnauzer, lay sprawled on the living room carpet, watching us.

"Come here, Benji." He dragged himself up, sauntered in and stood beside Sam, who drooled at the new top I now wriggled toward Benji.

"Sit." Benji hesitated, sat and gazed down, frowning. Benji doesn't respond to fruit rewards—only meat. He's picky. Sam performs for anything, including rawhides, dog food, broccoli, and carrots.

As with pets, we may become impatient with people who are particular. A frustrated friend of mine has tried for years to get her preschooler to eat more foods. Recently, she stumbled upon an answer—his fish tank.

"If you eat this, I will get you another fish."

"Really, Mom?" His eyes lit up. Now, they have visited the aquarium shop two weekends in a row.

Sometimes pets or people we love and live with challenge us daily because we don't know how to change them. We need to accept them as they are and learn how to work with their uniqueness.

Lord, help me to relinquish control to you when I cannot change others and feel irritated. Grant me acceptance and appreciation for who they are.

Rescued

We found Sarah on the side of the road, inside a deer that had been hit by a car. She was starved, and trying to take advantage of the free meal. Disgustingly dirty, she smelled worse than any dump I've ever been near.

She didn't resist when we tried to rescue her. Fortunately we had a truck, so we put her in the back and drove home, where we held our breaths to keep from gagging while we hosed her down, shampooed her, dried her off, and gave her a decent meal. Much to our delight, after all that filth was cleared away, she was a silky white ball of fluff with large, round eyes and a tail that wagged like nobody's business. We bought her a collar, some dog food, a couple dog bowls, and made her our own.

Sarah is a great reminder that God found me in a disgusting state, covered in the sin and filth of this world. Through Christ, He rescued us. When we trust Him and don't resist, He cleans us off, gives us new clothes, makes sure we have what we need, and makes us a member of the family. Why would we ever resist that kind of grace?

**Dear Father, Thank You for rescuing me.
Help me to live in gratitude of Your love.**

Forewarned Is Forearmed

These things happened to them as examples and were
written down as warnings for us, on whom the
culmination of the ages has come.

1 CORINTHIANS 10:11 NIV

Hans, a German shepherd who served alongside Bob in the
Vietnam War, very rarely barked. Hans had been trained as a scout
dog and he did his job masterfully. On any reconnaissance mission,
Hans never barked a warning. The fur on the back of his head and
his back stood as tall as a Buckingham Palace guard. With his nose
he pointed at danger's presence.

Bob trusted his scout dog completely and Hans never let him
down. Both survived the war and returned home as heroes.

The Word of God gives us ample warnings—warnings we
can trust. We are warned about making presumptions (Numbers
14:39–45). We are warned to always be on the alert for Satan's tricks
and subtlety (1 Peter 5:8 NLT). We are warned to follow after God
closely. When Peter asked Jesus about what would happen to John
in the future, Jesus replied, "What is that to you? You follow me"
(John 21:22 NLT).

Let's pay attention to God's warnings. God has given them to
us out of His overshadowing wisdom, love, and protection.

**Dear Father, help me pay attention to the warnings You give
me both in Your Word and through the wise advice of friends.**

So Much Joy—I Just Can't Contain It

And thou shalt rejoice before the LORD thy God, thou, and thy son,
and thy daughter, and thy manservant, and thy maidservant,
and the Levite that is within thy gates, and the stranger,
and the fatherless, and the widow, that are among you,
in the place which the LORD thy God hath
chosen to place his name there.

DEUTERONOMY 16:11 KJV

One afternoon I sat on my aunt's front porch with Suki, her miniature Alaskan shepherd. I noticed that as Suki sat in the cool grass, she seemed a little anxious. I guessed she was waiting for my uncle to get home from work.

The minute Suki saw his truck coming down the road, she darted toward his truck, which scared me a little at first. Then, as if an invisible fence held her prisoner, she ran back and forth across the yard, unable to contain her energy and excitement upon his arrival.

My uncle unexpectedly stopped his truck and Suki ran in circles around it until he opened his door and she jumped inside.

My uncle had a big grin on his face as he walked toward me with Suki right at his heels. "She's so excited to see me, she can't contain herself. I always reward her with a ride in the truck."

Father, fill me with excitement and anticipation as I spend time with You. I want to be so overflowing with joy in Your presence that I just can't contain it.

Bessie's First Christmas

Seek the LORD and His strength; seek His face evermore!
Remember His marvelous works which He has done.

PSALM 105:4–5 NKJV

Bessie the puppy was experiencing the first Christmas tree of her life. Roz had spent a delightful three hours Sunday night decorating it to artistic perfection. She loved how it turned out and made sure it was precisely centered in the front window for others to enjoy, as well. Bessie was also excited, but in a different way.

She had behaved perfectly fine around the tree with Roz and Ryan, so it seemed safe to leave her alone with the tree while they went off to work the next day. But on Monday evening Roz returned home to find the tree on its side, ornaments everywhere, branches and lights chewed off. Bessie had to have shocked herself in the process!

Roz was so frustrated with her. The following day, even with a barrier, Bessie managed to mangle the tree again. It was in ruins. All of that hard work for nothing! Or was it?

Roz was reminded that Christmas wasn't about a tree, or lights, or the way her house was decorated. It's all about Christ's birth and our freedom in Him. Sometimes you need your dog to tear down your Christmas tree to remember the greatest of realities.

**Lord, thank You for reminding me of the truth
and what truly matters in this life today and every day.**

Wait Patiently

We also pray that you will be strengthened with all his glorious power so you will have all the endurance and patience you need. May you be filled with joy.

COLOSSIANS 1:11 NLT

While I washed dishes, I noticed our neighbor's dog, Jake, sitting near his house, staring straight up. My eyes followed where his nose pointed to a squirrel clinging to the stucco near the eaves. Neither animal moved for several moments. Then the squirrel scrambled a few feet to one side and Jake changed his position to stay right below his prey. He wagged his tail and trembled with anticipation. Whether he envisioned a meal or a playmate, I didn't know.

The game continued all the time I cleaned the kitchen. Whenever the squirrel moved, Jake danced back and forth to be in the correct spot on the ground. The dog's endurance was surprising, as was the squirrel's perseverance.

I began to think of other things I needed to do, and was about to leave when the squirrel scurried down a few feet. Jake stood on his hind legs. Suddenly the squirrel leaped off the wall, landed behind Jake, and took off in a lightning-fast run. By the time Jake turned around, the squirrel was long gone. Instead of acting disappointed, Jake just shook himself and pranced off.

Maybe God was trying to show me something.

Heavenly Father, teach me to wait patiently, but not to be discouraged when Your plans are different from mine.

With You

Yet I am always with you; you hold me by my right hand.
You guide me with your counsel, and afterward you
will take me into glory.
PSALM 73:23–24 NIV

My grandmother always had dogs when I was growing up. But two particular dogs stand out in my memory. At one point she had an older Scottish terrier and a younger Cairn terrier. As the Scottie grew older, he slowly began to lose his eyesight. So, every morning before going downstairs for breakfast, the Cairn would wait at the top of the staircase for the Scottie and walk down next to him so that he wouldn't be scared of the stairs. She was his faithful companion, guide, and eyes.

You have an even more faithful Companion and Guide. God is always with you. Even in the darkest and loneliest moments, He is by your side. When everyone else has abandoned you, He continues to lead and guide you.

My grandmother's Scottie dog couldn't see the first step in front of him and so he relied on the presence of his friend to safely navigate the stairs. Similarly, when you feel that complete darkness has descended and you can't see far enough to take one more step, God holds your hand so you're not alone. Lean on Him to guide you in that next step.

You are my Lord and Guide. You will lead me in this life and hold my hand through to the next.

Can You Take My Dog?

He could also speak about animals, birds, small creatures, and fish.
And kings from every nation sent their ambassadors
to listen to the wisdom of Solomon.

1 KINGS 4:33–34 NLT

Sometimes I wish I could call upon the wisdom of Solomon, especially when a friend or acquaintance asks me, "You have dogs. My mom is going into a nursing home. My son is allergic to dog hair. Would you be willing to take Lady for us?"

Goodness. I love animals as much as anyone and want to see all pets in happy homes. I know the person who asks a favor like this is going through a tough time, transitioning someone to a nursing home and trying to find a forever home for a pet. But it's not fair to me, my family, or my own group of dogs. We have constraints on our time. A newcomer will bring maintenance and vet fees. There may be health or behavior issues. My dogs may not accept the new arrival.

In cases like this, I promise to call the Pet Ministry at my church. They're a great group and many churches have developed a similar help ministry for owners who can no longer care for or feed their pets. They collect donations to buy animal food for owners who are going through financial problems. They have volunteers who have signed up on a waiting list to take pets into their homes.

Lord, help us be sensitive to even the smallest
of needs of fellow pet owners.

T.J.'s Choice

Do not rejoice. . .do not be jubilant. . .
for you have been unfaithful.
HOSEA 9:1 NIV

I had never seen a long-haired Chihuahua before meeting T.J. She may have been cute and fluffy, but T.J. lacked the heroic tendencies found in dogs that star in made-for-TV movies. She wouldn't follow commands. She thought bugs were candy. If T.J. was human, she would have been a rebel.

I'd like to say that T.J. responded well to love and grace, that she recovered from her rebellion, and that she learned obedience. She didn't.

Not every person we know will make good choices just because we want them to. Even if we can change their behavior, we can only influence a rebellious heart.

We should pray to the God who promises in Ezekiel 36:26, "I will give you a new heart and put a new spirit in you; I will remove from you your heart of stone and give you a heart of flesh" (NIV).

We should provide an atmosphere of love and grace, but we must remember two things: Only God can change a heart, and each of us must make our own choices.

Dear God, help me to model godly behavior for my family. Help me follow You with all that I am. Then help me realize I'm ultimately responsible only for my own choices. For those who are in rebellion to You, please show them what life is like with You. Change their hearts and bring them home.

Healing Words

Gracious words are a honeycomb,
sweet to the soul and healing to the bones.
PROVERBS 16:24 NIV

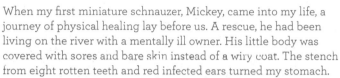

When my first miniature schnauzer, Mickey, came into my life, a journey of physical healing lay before us. A rescue, he had been living on the river with a mentally ill owner. His little body was covered with sores and bare skin instead of a wiry coat. The stench from eight rotten teeth and red infected ears turned my stomach.

However, his brave demeanor intrigued everyone—especially me. He seemed to plow through hardship and survive.

He learned to accept the cumbersome treatment collar he would wear for months, even though it interfered with his independent personality. He never seemed defeated. . .until his operation for an un-descended testicle, a benign tumor, and the removal of eight teeth occurred all on the same day.

When I brought him home from this mammoth surgery and general anesthesia, Mickey was miserable. His second post-op day, I shared my concern with a cat-loving friend on the phone.

"He's so listless. He barely looks at me. I can't get him to eat or drink water."

"Tell him you love him and need him to get better. Stroke him and hold his head so you are looking in his eyes."

I hung up the phone and frequently did as she described for the next forty-eight hours.

He revived.

Lord, help me to encourage those struggling
or suffering through loving words.

Protector

*"But the Lord is faithful, and he will strengthen you
and protect you from the evil one."*

2 THESSALONIANS 3:3 NIV

Jack, a rescue dog, had a sweet temperament. He would wag his tail, would roll over for belly rubs, and seemed to have a permanent smile on his face. It didn't take him long, after coming home from the shelter, to become attached to his new family. They thought he was just a laid-back, low-key pet until a salesman came to the door.

Jack sat in front of his owner, haunches raised, growling like a mama bear protecting her cubs. It didn't matter how many times his owner told him to stop. Jack insisted on making his intentions clear to the stranger: "You hurt my people, you'll pay the price."

In much the same way, God is our Protector. Though He is loving and compassionate, He is also fierce. When we accept His Son as our Savior, we become part of His family, and He takes family ties very seriously. Though He doesn't prevent every bad thing from coming our way, we may never know the harm that might have come to us without God's protection. When our enemy does attack, he does so with the knowledge that he will face God, and he'll have a heavy price to pay.

Dear Father, thank You for Your protection. When bad things happen, help me remember that You are on my side.

Miracles

You are the God of great wonders!
PSALM 77:14 NLT

"Cheerio!" Nancy opened her back door and called for her aging, blind Cockapoo. She had let Cheerio out, but then her toddling grandson kept her absorbed. When Nancy finally returned to the door to let Cheerio back in, her dog was gone.

Nancy quickly put her grandson in his crib and went outside to find Cheerio. She called and searched to no avail. After hours had passed, daylight slipped into darkness. Still no Cheerio. The family spread out all over their spacious property, praying, calling, and searching with lights. The wind had continued to blow and snow covered any tracks. Despite going to neighbors and posting information and a call for help on social media, no one had seen the little dog.

That night passed. And another. And another. The daytime temperatures barely made it to zero. At night the temperatures were more than fifteen degrees *below* zero.

Finally, a friend of a friend on Facebook found Cheerio in the woods and returned her. Cheerio reeked of deer urine, she had lost weight, and her body temperature was low, but the veterinarian pronounced Cheerio well enough to return home. She's still going strong a year later.

Many dismiss miracles, but our God specializes in them—big and small, far reaching and close at hand. Be ready for a miracle when you least expect it.

**Almighty God, You are the God of miracles.
All praise to You!**

You Are Accepted and Welcomed

And let us consider one another in order to stir up love and
good works, not forsaking the assembling of ourselves together,
as is the manner of some, but exhorting one another,
and so much the more as you see the Day approaching.
HEBREWS 10:24–25 NKJV

Chris and Angela's move from the Arizona desert to the Midwest
left them wondering how their dog, Toby, would adjust. He had
never seen grass, leaves, or snow. Toby rejoiced at the first trip
into the grassy backyard. Angela could tell the new smells were
like candy to his nose. He ran back and forth through the grass,
stopping every so often to roll around in the grass for a few seconds.

During their first walk through the neighborhood with Toby,
they met a few neighbors. One neighbor in particular came out
with a bacon dog treat in hand. He asked for permission and then
presented Toby with the gift. "I love dogs," the older man quipped.
"Every dog in the neighborhood knows my house. All dogs are
welcomed. And the treats keep them coming back for more." He
laughed.

Moving and leaving all their friends and family was difficult for
Chris and Angela, but they knew this was where the Lord wanted
them. This was the first of many new experiences in which they felt
accepted and welcomed.

Lord, thank You for placing people in my life
who love, accept, and welcome me.

Artful

Rest in the LORD, and wait patiently for Him;
do not fret because of him who prospers in his way.
PSALM 37:7 NKJV

Bessie's favorite pastime is toilet-papering the house. If the bathroom door is left open, she will sneak in ever so quietly and carefully grab the end of the toilet paper roll. She slowly unravels the roll and pulls it all over the house. This happens at least two or three times a week for Roz and Ryan. One time Roz was in the laundry room for about five minutes. She walked into the living room and found Bessie in the middle of a giant web of toilet paper. She had unraveled an entire brand-new roll of toilet paper. Roz has learned to smile about it—and to shut the bathroom door.

You do what you can, but sometimes you just have to embrace the chaos and enjoy the art of gracefully draped toilet paper over every piece of furniture in the living room.

Lord God, in the mayhem that can be a day, give me the grace to relax in the moments that are literally unraveling. Help me to rest in You no matter what.

You're My Family

To redeem them that were under the law,
that we might receive the adoption of sons.
GALATIANS 4:5 KJV

My husband was in the navy, stationed at China Lake, California. We lived in military housing, and sometimes previous tenants left property behind when they moved. For our neighbors, Lew and Mary, the abandoned item was a very large, brownish dog. As soon as they moved in, he adopted them as his family. They named him Flip and started an interesting relationship.

Flip's pedigree was definitely not pure—just big. When he came inside our little houses, one wag of his tail sent items flying from coffee tables, and anything on the floor was trampled.

He became a self-proclaimed guardian to anyone he thought needed protection, which was reassuring when the men were on duty at night. We knew Flip was gentle, but he had a fierce growl.

Mary and I often went to the commissary together and usually found Flip waiting for us at the door before we got there. We never understood how he knew where we were going, but the 15-mile-per-hour speed limit on the base caused us to arrive later than him. We took turns shopping, while one of us stayed with Flip in the parking lot. His habits could be annoying, but his love was irresistible.

**Father, Your Word says You adopt us into Your family.
You accept us just as we are, and allow us to
thrive in the safety of Your love.**

Follow My Example

Follow my example, as I follow the example of Christ.
1 CORINTHIANS 11:1 NIV

Willow is a giant schnauzer whose best friend is a very petite dachsund/Papillon mix named Luna. Luna was still a puppy when she first met Willow, and from the very beginning was clearly impressed with Willow and emulated her in everything she did. When she comes to visit, Luna won't eat unless her bowl is right next to Willow's. On walks, Luna will run around chaotically, smelling everything and walking in front of whoever is walking her. But if you put her next to Willow she immediately calms down and walks perfectly on the leash as Willow has been trained to do.

Do you have a Willow in your life—someone to learn from and emulate? Do you know someone who you respect so much that you desire to walk through life with the same poise, grace, humor, and faith as they do? It's important to have a Willow, someone who is following Christ so closely that emulating them will inevitably make you more Christlike.

As you grow in your knowledge and love of Christ, look for a Luna—someone whom you can impact and encourage to grow in their faith.

It's a beautiful thing to be in the Body of Christ, where you have the blessing of both being encouraged and being an encouragement.

Lord, give me the grace and privilege of having a close relationship with someone who knows and loves You well so that I can become more like You by emulating them. In turn, help me to seek out those whom I can encourage, as well.

Sticky Situation

If we confess our sins, he is faithful and just and will forgive us our sins and purify us from all unrighteousness.

1 JOHN 1:9 NIV

Some say that dogs are good judges of character. We thought so of our dog, Duppy. Like most dogs, Duppy was protective of her food and water bowls. The only place we had room for them in our small home was near the door. She didn't trust people, so when someone came to the door, she would grab her food and water bowls and take them somewhere else in the house.

One day (I don't know whose brilliant idea it was) my sisters and I put cola in her water dish to see if she'd drink it. She didn't. Before we could empty the bowl, one of our friends with a loud voice came to the door. Duppy grabbed her bowl of cola and took it into the living room, jumping up onto one of the comfy chairs and spilling cola all over it. We had a hard time explaining how the dog dumped pop all over the living room chair. Nevertheless, our mother helped us clean up the mess.

When we find ourselves in sticky situations, it's best to come clean to God, so He can help to clean us up. He is the only One who can.

Lord, I am so thankful that when I confess my sin, You are quick to forgive me and cleanse my soul.

Powerful Words

A person finds joy in giving an apt reply—
and how good is a timely word!
PROVERBS 15:23 NIV

There are three powerful words in our dog's listening vocabulary: "Walk," "Food," and "Treat." These words are so effective because we use them sparingly, even among the human members of the family. If we don't intend for the dogs to accompany us, we say we are going for a "stroll." I cook "meals" for the family, and ice cream is a "dessert." We have had good results with the power words, since the dogs always know there is a pleasant event in the near future when we say them. Jot jumps at her leash when she hears the word "walk," and Tilly spins in circles if anyone even whispers, "Food." The most powerful word is saved for the most important time. All of our dogs have squeezed through the fence or darted out the front door at some time or other. Whistling, calling their names, and chasing them only seem to add to their fun as they race across the neighbors' yards. The only surefire way to bring them back to safety is to use the most powerful word: "TREAT!"

God has spoken to us through His Word, the Bible. In it we find all the power we need. His Word feeds us, shows us the path we should take, and brings us back to Him when we stray.

Lord, open my ears to Your holy Word.
I will listen to You today.

Want

Turn my eyes away from worthless things;
preserve my life according to your word.
PSALM 119:37 NIV

I tossed two bones to Benji, my mini-schnauzer, and Sam, my Lab. Benji promptly dropped his bone and snatched Sam's right out of his mouth. Sam stared into his little brother's fiery eyes before Benji trotted off.

I threw Sam another rawhide.

Immediately, Benji dropped the last bone he stole from Sam and ran back to him, snarling. Sam turned away, gripping his treat. Benji growled and nipped Sam's giant paw. He wanted that bone.

My dad frowned. "Is he always like this?"

"Benji wants whatever Sammy has." I rolled my eyes. "It doesn't matter if they each get treats. He only wants what belongs to Sam."

Benji is a grabby little guy when he's in the *want mode*. It's all about him.

People can be ugly, too, sometimes. They are ungrateful for what they have, focused only on what they lack. God wisely commands us not to covet our neighbor's goods or crave their possessions but to be thankful for what we have.

God loves us, just as I love Benji—no matter how ornery, unkind, and unholy we can be. His love reflects the patient instruction of a long-suffering parent. He attempts to extract the best virtue while working with the worst—accepting us, while instructing us. . .much the way we try to train our pets.

Father, guard me from greed. I choose to want less rather than have more. Help me to cultivate a garden of gratefulness.

Bad Day

The Lord disciplines the one he loves.
HEBREWS 12:6 NIV

Ginger had a bad day yesterday. First, she chewed my phone charger in half when she was riding in my car. I didn't realize until too late why she was so quiet. Now she's been banned from riding in the car with me until she's out of her puppy-chewing stage.

Then she got caught chasing our chickens. From the time we brought her home, we've allowed her to be around our birds, hoping she'd see them as family members, not food. I do believe she just wanted to play, but I had to scold her and put her in her kennel for a while.

I'm not angry at Ginger. She's a puppy, doing puppy things. But as her master, it's my job to teach her. That phone charger could have choked her. And if she becomes aggressive with our birds, we'll have to find her a new home.

Sometimes we make mistakes, not out of rebellion, but just because we're human and we mess up. When that happens, God doesn't become angry. He does discipline us, though. His discipline happens because He loves us, and He wants to teach us the right way to live. He wants to prevent bad things from seeping into our lives and harming us. When we feel the sting of His discipline, we need to remind ourselves He's not upset with us. He simply loves us and wants to keep us safe.

**Dear Father, thank You for Your discipline.
I know it's a sign of Your love for me.**

Today's Menu Selection Includes. . .

You must give an account on judgment day
for every idle word you speak.
MATTHEW 12:36 NLT

Mike and Sue came home to an unpleasant surprise. They had attended a series of meetings on another island in Indonesia, where they live. While they were gone, their dog, Heidi, had run away.

Heidi, an indiscriminate mix of canine breeds, is a good-sized dog with floppy ears and a sweet face and personality. Where she was, they had no idea, but the search was on as soon as they returned home.

Fortunately, one of their helpers found their dog just in time. Some street children had captured Heidi and sold her for $72 to a restaurant owner. The owner did not buy Heidi for a watchdog or a pet, but for something he regularly offers at his restaurant, a dish called *rintek wuuk*: dog meat.

Some people of Jesus' day had rules about what they put into their mouths. Even today some people will only eat vegan, vegetarian, halal, or kosher. The Lord told those willing to listen, however, that what comes out of a person's mouth is what defiles him (Matthew 15:11). We must be more diligent about what comes out of our mouths than what goes into them. As the old children's song reminds us, "Be careful, little mouth, what you say."

Lord God, I pray to be careful in all I say today.

Spiritual Makeover

We were therefore buried with him through baptism into death in order that, just as Christ was raised from the dead through the glory of the Father, we too may live a new life.

ROMANS 6:4 NIV

Rachel texted her daughter, Lizzie—ON THE WAY HOME FROM THE GROOMER WITH ALLY. Lizzie shared the news with her sister, Claire. The girls positioned themselves on the couch in the game room, waiting for Ally, their Scottie, to bounce into the house.

"It's so funny how Ally runs and hides when she knows she's going to the groomer, but then she's all like, 'look at me,' when she gets here," said Claire.

"She definitely loves the attention. It's good for us to make a big deal over her when she gets home—that way she knows we are proud of her," replied Rachel.

Ally bounded into the game room and then stopped right in front of the girls as if to say, "I'm here!" She waited, anxiously wagging her tail. The girls each squealed with delight and showered her with words of praise for several minutes, touching her bows and giving her hugs and kisses.

Jesus, thank You for my spiritual makeover. I look good in Christ because You have forgiven me for my sins and made me completely new. When people look at me, I pray they see You!

The Dog Ate It

*Then our mouth was filled with laughter, and our tongue
with singing. Then they said among the nations,
"The Lord has done great things for them."*

PSALM 126:2 NKJV

According to some students, dogs eat homework. Roz's dog, Bessie,
favored a different school-themed treat. Roz, a school counselor,
isn't sure she will ever live this story down.

Her ID badge was in her coat pocket, where she kept it each
night until she needed to put it on again for work the next day. That
evening she put food in Bessie's bowl, and then went about getting
things ready for her own dinner. She could hear Bessie chewing as
she cooked, and assumed she was eating her food. When she turned
around, she was surprised to find Bessie's food untouched—Roz's
mandatory work ID badge was the main focus of the chomping
attention. That was an awkward conversation to have with her
principal the next morning at school. The story brought plenty of
laughter, and whenever it is retold at school or on social media, it
still gets a good chuckle.

**God, thanks for laughter! Even when the things that make me
laugh are often initially very frustrating, I am so grateful
when You lift my spirit with good humor.**

Why Aren't You Grateful?

Therefore, since we are receiving a kingdom that cannot be shaken,
let us be thankful, and so worship God acceptably
with reverence and awe.

HEBREWS 12:28 NIV

When my family first brought Willow home from the shelter, she was a big, goofy, lovable dog with a *major* defiant streak. She had not been taught any manners by her previous owners and was, therefore, a very difficult dog.

On one occasion when she was being particularly disobedient, I got down on the ground, held her big head in my hands, and said, "Willow, we rescued you from an uncertain future in a scary shelter and brought you here, where we take care of your every need and love you and sacrifice time and money for you—why aren't you grateful?"

I was immediately struck by my own words.

Why am *I* not grateful? Christ saved me from certain death, washed away my sins with His own blood, justified me, and adopted me into His family, where He loves me with a perfect, undefiled love. Instead of being grateful, I live a life where I'm the priority, where I defiantly act as though I don't need God by nonchalantly choosing worthless things over my time with Him. I pray as though He owes me something instead of the other way around. I minimize the sacrifice of His Son on the cross by repeatedly going back to the sins that He bled for. And yet He still loves me fiercely and will never give up on me.

Why am *I* not grateful?

Lord, I worship You with reverence
and awe for what You have done for me.

Adoption

I remember clearly the dogs of our country neighborhood when I
was a kid. My family had Duppy, a rat terrier mix, black with tan
eyebrows. Our neighbors had Sparkie, also a terrier mix, not much
bigger than a football with short legs. My aunt's dog, Blondie, was a
blond cocker spaniel. My other aunt had Blondie's red-furred sister,
Sandy.

One time Duppy and Sandy each had a litter of puppies.
Duppy developed a condition that when the puppies nursed, they
drained all the energy and nutrition from her. It wasn't long before
Duppy couldn't walk. In desperation, we took all of Duppy's puppies
to Sandy, hoping she would accept them. My cousins were proud
and we were grateful when Sandy readily accepted the new puppies.

Adoption can be a wonderful thing. And how wonderful it is
that God adopted us into His family. As children of God, we are
His beneficiaries. In Jesus we receive righteousness, forgiveness,
salvation, eternal life, and the right to come boldly to the throne of
grace.

**Father, thank You that through Your great love
and the sacrifice of Your Son, I am Your child,
and I will live with You eternally in heaven.**

Divine Watch Dog

*"Because he loves me," says the LORD, "I will rescue him;
I will protect him, for he acknowledges my name."*

PSALM 91:14 NIV

Grace and her curly canine buddy, Smokey, traveled to a campground hours away.

Another great outing! The widow smiled at the motor homes and campers around her as she set up her campsite in a rural area. *No one will know I'm alone.*

But as Sunday afternoon waned, campers left. Hers was the only tent in the campsite loop.

Then a man drove up and scanned her campsite, seeing one of each: chair, place setting at the table, tent, and sleeping bag. Grace realized her mistake as he initiated conversation and demands.

While she prayed for God's help, Smokey lunged at the stranger, snarling and barking.

"Call off your dog!"

"She bites. If you need camping gear like you said, you'll have to get it in town."

As the man left, Grace smiled at Smokey.

Fear and anxiety comes for many reasons—physical threats, a disturbing diagnosis, financial crises, catastrophe, or the death of loved ones.

A recent study showed that 85 percent of what people worry about never happens, and of that which does, 79 percent of people reported they handled the situation better than they expected or they learned an invaluable lesson. But turning the worry over to God is even better. He protects us and shows the way.

**Thank You, Lord, for conquering my worries
and being my Protector.**

Passing Through

You are better off to have a friend than to be all alone.
ECCLESIASTES 4:9 CEV

In my state, a lost dog can go to a new owner if the previous owner cannot be located within thirty days. That's how I came to befriend Bufford. He was loving, kind, and loud. If something captured his attention, he tried to ensure that people three states away knew it. The neighbors were not kind in their new pet assessment.

In time there came a call from a man who knew every marking on Bufford. He knew Bufford was not the dog's name. He knew Bufford was lost in a hunting expedition. He knew he wanted his dog back.

When the man came from another state it was easy to see that Bufford knew, loved, and missed his owner. My neighbors wouldn't miss Bufford, but it was hard for me to see him go.

God designed us for relationships, which explains why we want friends, family, and dogs. There is comfort in sharing life with others. Some stick around for a long time. Others make an impact and move along. But the One who has always been by your side is the One who made you. Get to know Him. He's not going anywhere.

Dear God, You've never wanted me to be lonely. Even when I'm alone I have You. I can talk to You any time and Your words are always available to comfort me. I'm glad companionship was Your idea. I think it's one of Your best.

Stop and Watch the Clouds

The heavens declare the glory of God;
the skies proclaim the work of his hands.

PSALM 19:1 NIV

Benji, my miniature schnauzer, often sits very still and quiet for long periods of time. Whether he's at the sofa window, sliding back door, the car console, or leashed—he waits and watches to detect movement. His head rivets from side to side, and his eyes dart like a chipmunk. We laugh when his ears spring to new heights and he barks. He's the first to spot people, dogs, squirrels, birds, even mice!

I do not often stay in one place long enough to observe my surroundings as Benji does. I like to move—not watch movement.

Recently, on vacation in Missoula, my husband set his cell phone to time-lapse video and anchored it to the car window with the lid to our ice bucket. I laughed.

"We will see the clouds moving every five seconds," he joyfully explained.

"I already took pictures of clouded blue skies this trip," I answered, amused, before scurrying off to walk the nearby trails. When I returned, we watched the results of his extended efforts of observation. Peering into the cell phone screen, discovery and incomparable delight unexpectedly gripped us. Exhilaration flared as we watched nature's live display. Clouds, sometimes swirling, sometimes waltzing, morphed into amazing, varied formations over the Montana mountains. Hanging clouds are pretty, but moving clouds are breathtaking.

Slow me down, Lord, to see the wonder in nature today.

Excited

Come, everyone! Clap your hands!
Shout to God with joyful praise!
PSALM 47:1 NLT

Sometimes it seems like Moses has a split personality. When I've been gone, he welcomes me home with such over-the-top, obnoxious excitement, I can't even get in the door. That behavior is cute for about ten seconds before it becomes downright annoying. When he gets all riled up, it sometimes takes the better part of an hour to calm him down.

One time, he was still really excited after I came home, fixed some popcorn, and settled on the couch for some downtime. He jumped smack-dab in the middle of my lap, sending popcorn flying everywhere. Months later, I'm still finding popcorn in nooks and crannies.

Other times, though, when I stay close to home, Moses simply goes to sleep at my feet. On those days, there's no sign of his out-of-control hyperactive nonsense.

While I get annoyed at Moses' joy, it also warms my heart that he misses me so much. One big difference between God and me is that God never, ever gets annoyed because I'm excited to be in His presence. As a matter of fact, He delights in my joy.

He loves it when I celebrate Him, and He loves it when I rest at His feet. He longs for me to adore Him the way Moses adores me.

Dear Father, I'm so grateful to be Your child.
Help me to celebrate Your presence and rest at Your feet.

The Fallen Hero

God demonstrates his own love for us in this:
While we were still sinners, Christ died for us.
ROMANS 5:8 NIV

On a hot August night, K-9 officer Falko and his partner, police officer Samantha Snowberger, approached a vacant house in pursuit of two armed suspects. The two police officers entered the house; Falko was shot and his human officer returned fire. To Samantha's great sorrow, her faithful and well-loved partner died at the scene.

Falko had no suspicion of his impending death when he entered that house. He was simply doing his job: pursuing suspected felons. The pursuit ended badly for all. One of the suspects died, Falko died, and Samantha and the other suspect both lost their best friends.

Unlike Falko, Jesus knew all that awaited Him. He not only understood it, but He purposely went to death. Christ "resolutely set out for Jerusalem" (Luke 9:51 NIV). "I lay down my life for the sheep," He said. "I lay it down of my own accord" (John 10:15, 18).

Jesus Christ *willingly* laid down His life to save us from death and sin. He did this for everyone: you and me, felons and grieving police officers. There is no greater love than this.

Lord, how can I begin to thank You for Your sacrifice for me?
Forgive me for my sin against You. Be not my partner,
but the Master of my life.

Jesus Healed Them All

News about him spread as far as Syria, and people soon began bringing to him all who were sick. And whatever their sickness or disease, or if they were demon possessed or epileptic or paralyzed—he healed them all.

MATTHEW 4:24 NLT

No matter how many times I asked him not to, my husband, Blaine, continued to play golf in the house. Our dog, Romeo, loved to chase the balls. Late one evening I heard a horrible yelp and rushed to find Romeo on the floor, motionless. Romeo had run toward the ball just as Blaine swung the golf club, hitting him in the jaw.

In my pajamas and house shoes, I scooped up our little baby and headed to the car. We rushed to the animal hospital—thankfully one was just a few minutes from our house. I prayed the whole way. Just as we pulled into the parking spot, I felt Romeo come alive. Before that movement, I didn't think he was breathing, but I prayed God would heal him and make him whole—and He did.

By the time we reached the doctor, Romeo was awake and walking around as if nothing had happened. They checked him over thoroughly and let us take him home. Relieved and truly grateful for God's healing hand, we returned home.

Heavenly Father, thank You for Your healing power at work in our lives. You perfect that which concerns us. Keep me and all those I love in perfect health.

Making the Rounds

*I, the L*ORD*, search the heart, I test the mind, even to give every man according to his ways, according to the fruit of his doings.*
JEREMIAH 17:10 NKJV

Frank's wet nose nuzzled me awake. I saw his concerned brown eyes brighten as I picked my head up and rubbed his kiss off my cheek. When he saw I was all right, he turned to run off. His work there was done. Now he would make his way through each open door of the house and whine softly at the unopened ones. We are his people, and he was doing his usual job of making sure we were all okay.

What a blessing it is to be cared for, to see such concern exhibited for me. Yet isn't this precisely what God does for you and me every moment of every day? He sees. He waits. He looks me in the eye. He sees far beyond what my dog can—He sees my heart and knows exactly what I need.

Lord God, I am so glad You know more than just my immediate needs. You know the intricacies of my complex heart and mind. Give me what You know I need today for wholeness in You.

Secret Place

*He who dwells in the secret place of the Most High
shall abide under the shadow of the Almighty.*

PSALM 91:1 NKJV

Misty, our tan and white cocker spaniel, gave birth to three puppies.
They were housed in a big, cozy box lined with soft blankets. Our
children loved to gently pet the newborns and watch as Misty cared
for her family.

We had a fenced backyard, so Misty could go outside without
supervision and was always eager to get back in. But one day, when
the puppies were about two weeks old, she stayed out longer than
usual and the little ones were making hungry noises. I went to the
back door, expecting her to be there waiting, but there was no sign
of her. I called. No response.

We began to search the neighborhood to see if she had
somehow gotten out of the yard. Then we did a more thorough
investigation in the backyard. We found her hiding in a hole she'd
dug under the shelter of a pine tree—a secret place for a temporary
escape.

I assured her, "Look, I totally understand that sometimes you
just want to get away for a bit. But your family needs you." As soon
as we discovered her, she came inside and was ready to resume her
responsibilities. She just needed a little break.

**Thank You, heavenly Father, for understanding our need
for a secret place. You refresh and protect us
when we hide in Your sheltering love.**

Hello There!

No one has ever seen God; but if we love one another,
God lives in us and his love is made complete in us.
1 JOHN 4:12 NIV

We've all had those days that leave us feeling totally defeated, worthless, and exhausted. But for dog lovers, there's at least one thing that's capable of cheering up even the roughest of days: walking through the front door to be accosted by the greeting of a devoted dog. With the tail wag that morphs into the full-body wiggle and the eyes that say "never leave again," a dog says "hello" in a way that lets you know that you are remarkably important and loved.

We would be wise to take a lesson from these pups who have mastered the art of saying "hello" by learning to enthusiastically greet our fellow humans (albeit with a little less wiggling involved).

A friendly and heartfelt greeting can speak volumes to someone who is lonely, suffering, or insecure. Simply letting a person know that you're happy to see them tells them that they are worthwhile, noticed, and known.

Loving others is a tangible representation of God. Though we won't see God in this life, we can see His love in one another. So don't underestimate the power of an enthusiastic and loving greeting, for through it shines the face of God.

Lord, give me opportunities to share Your love with those
around me, whether they are close friends or strangers.
Don't let my own insecurities or shyness serve as
an excuse to leave a greeting unsaid.

Waiting at the Door

*Here I am! I stand at the door and knock. If anyone hears
my voice and opens the door, I will come in and eat
with that person, and they with me.*

"John, look," said Jeanette, as she pointed to the stray on the porch.
The wide irrigation canal and a gate separated their state park
house from intruders—except for one.

"That scruffy dog slept on the porch again last night with
Dutch. When it's time to lock the gate, do you want me to lock the
other dog out?"

They studied the caramel-colored mutt. He snuggled next to
their dog. Dutch sleepily wiggled his eyebrows, then curled up in a
contented ball.

"Jeanette, why bother? That dog has been swimming the canal
to get here every night for a week. I think he wants to stay. I say we
name him."

After Gus became part of the family, he only swam the canal
for fun.

The invitation for Jesus to come into our lives is a gentle
nudge. He is patient. We can choose. God's motivation is real love
for us. Jesus opens the door to heaven and to His family. When our
Christian walk becomes calloused, dusty, and predictable, we can
accept His invitation anew. Want to grow to your full potential?
Ask. See His doors open wide.

My Savior, I open the door to You for my journey. I am willing.

Bringing Baron Home

In peace I will lie down and sleep, for you alone,
O LORD, will keep me safe.
PSALM 4:8 NLT

My family went through three German shepherds from the time I was a baby until I went off to college. The first one lived until I was twelve. My family didn't believe in waiting to get a replacement dog. "That's the only way to get over our grief," Mom said. Our house was so quiet and empty that we started contacting private breeders right away. I was old enough to be part of the process, and it was an adventure going out to different sellers in the area to check out their pups.

That's how we ended up choosing a three-month-old shepherd we named Baron. He was black-haired all over except for tan legs and small patches of tan on his face. Our first shepherd had been almost entirely tan and white, so this was something new for us. We didn't want the new dog to look just like the one we'd lost. We almost called him Blackie, but Dad said we had to give him a German name because he was a *German* shepherd. We called him Baron Ludwig and taught him commands like *"Schnell"* (Quick).

I cradled Baron in my arms, wrapped in a blanket, as Dad drove us home. We bonded while I kept him calm.

Lord, keep us in perfect peace, just as we transfer that sense of peace to the animals who depend upon us.

Merciful Misty

Let us come boldly to the throne of our gracious God.
There we will receive his mercy, and we will find
grace to help us when we need it most.

HEBREWS 4:16 NLT

Misty was a rescue puppy. When she came to live with my father-in-law, Lloyd, she was malnourished, mistreated, and without trust. He was a gentle giant suffering the relentless advance of Alzheimer's disease.

Misty understood him quickly and was a frequent guest on his lap for viewings of television Westerns. Her playful antics brought a smile to Lloyd's face, and her resting form invited him to rub behind her ears his unspoken affection.

She was Lloyd's dog even when he forgot her name. She didn't struggle with the awkwardness some felt around him. Lloyd's disease caused nothing to change between the two.

Misty was a gift of mercy to a man who needed it. She was the companion who was never embarrassed by or for her master. Misty never treated Lloyd as if he was defective. She reminds me of Jesus, who offers mercy, is a companion who forgives, and could view us without defect when He rescued us.

Dear God, You want me to accept Your mercy and pass it on to others. You want me to know I am accepted and loved while You invite me to grow and learn. I needed rescue and You rescued. You offered relationship and called me friend. You invited me to walk and carried me when I was weary. I'm overwhelmed by Your love.

Protection

For you alone, LORD, make me dwell in safety.
PSALM 4:8 NIV

"Don't come any closer!" I warned the unkempt stranger approaching me from our driveway.

"I'm just. . ." His words faded under Sam's large barks. Sam stood atop our front yard mound, hackles up, tail stiff and teeth shining.

"Okay, lady. . ." The man turned and walked on.

At the time, I was feeling vulnerable due to injuries that left me weak. When I bought Sam as a puppy, the owner assured me Sam's dad was a good guard dog. That day I was particularly thankful to God for giving me a protective Lab.

I thought of that incident recently when swimming alone in a hotel's indoor lap pool, frequently surfacing in my goggles to look around. The next day my husband accompanied me and worked while I swam. I could relax without feeling the need to monitor my surroundings. What a difference it made, knowing he was there.

In the Bible, young King David led armies to victory multiple times before a sudden twist of events found him alone in the Judean desert—hunted by an army of men. Weak and frightened, he cried out to God to be his defender and protector. He began gathering mighty warriors around him and wrote poems and songs that would comfort believers for centuries to come.

Are you in need of protection today?

Thank You, Lord, for Your daily protection I don't even realize is there, and for the people and animals You bring into my life as protectors.

Because I'm His

*"But God demonstrates his own love for us in this:
While we were still sinners, Christ died for us."*
ROMANS 5:8 NIV

Bo was a Basset hound. He was older when we got him, and all he did was eat, sleep, and. . .well, poop. He was every inch a Basset hound, from the stubby legs to the droopy eyes to the stereotypical hound-dog laziness. But to me, the nine-year-old girl who'd always wanted a dog of her own, he was perfect. I loved him just the way he was, because he was mine. I never gave up on trying to teach him tricks, even though he never learned any of them. To me, it was more about relationship than results.

God doesn't have any illusions about us. He knows we're sinful. He knows we're smelly and dirty, and some of us can be quite lazy when it comes to learning to walk with Him. Many days, quite honestly, it must seem we're more trouble than we're worth.

God loves us just the way we are, because we're His. He made us, and He wants us. He'll never stop caring for our needs, and He'll never give up on trying to teach us to be like Him, though He knows we'll never reach perfection. To Him, it's about relationship. The good news is, the closer our relationship with Him, the better the results.

Dear Father, thank You for loving me the way I am.
Thank You for never giving up on me. Help me to
become more like You each day.

A Rose by Any Other Name

And the disciples were called Christians first in Antioch.
ACTS 11:26 KJV

What do you think of when you hear the word *Trombiculidae*? How about "chiggers"?

Chiggers are a variety of mites called *Trombiculidae*. For years "Chiggers" was also the name of my favorite aunt and uncle's dog. I don't know how he got his name, but Chiggers was fun and romped with us kids.

The next time I ran into chiggers—the mites, not the dog—was when a nurse I worked with showed me her bites: nasty, itchy, red welts covering her stomach. I don't recall how she got them, but it made me wonder why my aunt and uncle ever named their dog "Chiggers."

Names are important in the Bible. When we are called by the name of Christ Jesus (Christians), we are to remember whose we are and conduct ourselves in light of that honorable Name. In the early days of the Church, "the name of the Lord Jesus was held in high honor" when the apostle Paul did not retreat from a demonic attack (Acts 19:17 NIV). Peter tells us, "If you suffer as a Christian. . .praise God that you bear that name" (1 Peter 4:16 NIV).

When others see us in the course of everyday life, let us never leave them wondering how we got the name "Christian."

**Dear Father, I pray I never bring shame
to the name of the Lord Christ.**

You're Worth It!

For God so loved the world, that he gave his only begotten Son,
that whosoever believeth in him should not perish,
but have everlasting life.

JOHN 3:16 KJV

Janna rolled over to turn off the alarm. She tried to remember why she'd set her alarm an hour earlier than normal. *Oh,* she thought, *I need to drop Muffin off at the groomers, and pick her up at lunchtime.* She looked at the nine-year-old, brown, long-haired dachshund burrowed under her blanket at the foot of her bed.

She thought once her children were out of the house, her responsibilities would diminish, but this dog—this creature she loved—seemed to take more and more time as she got older. When she was tempted to complain about the dog hair, the trips out in the rain and snow to scoop up poop, and the extra effort either to take the dog with her on trips or get a dog sitter, she remembered the unconditional love Muffin poured out.

"She's worth it," Janna said aloud as she wrapped her robe around her and slipped on her shoes to face the cool morning in order to take Muffin out to do her business. Deep in her heart, she felt the presence of the Lord say to her, "You're worth it to Me! I have loved you with an everlasting love."

Lord, thank You for considering me worth it.
Thank You for Your unfailing love!

Postpartum Zoey

The troubles of my heart have enlarged;
bring me out of my distresses!
PSALM 25:17 NKJV

Ten little Lab shepherd puppies squeaked and squealed around
Zoey as she tended to their every need. They awoke every hour or
two for a feeding frenzy, and afterward Zoey gave each of them a
bath before they fell back to sleep. Zoey was losing her hair and
a lot of weight, along with her sanity it seemed. On more than
one occasion she apparently had enough of it all and just started
walking away from the house, toward the busy road. One time
I spotted her from the window after she'd made it to the road. I
alerted my son, who tore out the front door barefoot across our
front yard beside the four hundred-foot driveway. "Zoey, come!"
Meanwhile I ran for the garage and started toward her in my car. We
managed to keep her alive and she managed to keep all the puppies
alive, but it sure wasn't easy working through the postpartum
doggie blues.

Lord, keep me steady in the ebb and flow of life's workload.
When I feel like running, tether me near to Your heart.

Able to Forgive

Get rid of all bitterness, rage and anger, brawling and slander, along with every form of malice. Be kind and compassionate to one another, forgiving each other, just as in Christ God forgave you.
EPHESIANS 4:31–32 NIV

When working with rescue dogs, it doesn't take long to be struck by their resiliency and capability to forgive.

Minnie was dangerously underweight and had been horribly mistreated by humans. . . .and yet, after being rescued, she got up to greet every person who walked in the door at the animal hospital as though each was her best friend. Devon had scars all over his face that spoke of his ruthless past. . .and yet, at adoption events, all he wanted from humans was a belly rub. Baloo came from an abusive past that was evidenced by how he cowered in the corner at the smallest sound or ducked his head if you lifted your hand to pet him too quickly. . .and yet, he would slowly slink over to a person to curl up next to them for some affection.

Why is it that we are so much less willing and eager to forgive? Sure, it's more complicated for humans. But maybe looking at forgiveness with a dog-like simplicity would be refreshing. Instead of holding on to a grudge that will ultimately hurt you more than it will hurt the person who wronged you, try forgiving and loving them instead. Don't allow wounds to fester into bitterness and harden into deep-seated cynicism. Instead, allow yourself the joy that comes with being kind and compassionate to others.

Lord, help me to forgive others as I have been completely and undeservedly forgiven by You.

Moon Shadow

But thanks be to God, who always leads us as captives in Christ's triumphal procession and uses us to spread the aroma of the knowledge of him everywhere.

2 CORINTHIANS 2:14 NIV

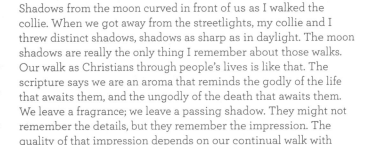

Shadows from the moon curved in front of us as I walked the collie. When we got away from the streetlights, my collie and I threw distinct shadows, shadows as sharp as in daylight. The moon shadows are really the only thing I remember about those walks. Our walk as Christians through people's lives is like that. The scripture says we are an aroma that reminds the godly of the life that awaits them, and the ungodly of the death that awaits them. We leave a fragrance; we leave a passing shadow. They might not remember the details, but they remember the impression. The quality of that impression depends on our continual walk with Jesus, so that we become His shadow, His aroma, passing among them.

If we're aware of Him, they'll be aware of Him. And they'll remember. When God visits them, they'll remember.

Lord, help me to relax as I walk each moment with You. Help me to sense Your presence; help me to walk as You walked, with love, truth, and honesty that sticks with people.

Big Enough

Are not two sparrows sold for a penny? Yet not one of them
will fall to the ground outside your Father's care.
MATTHEW 10:29 NIV

Shortly after my husband and I were married, I saw a Saint Bernard mix that I loved. In the following years, whenever we talked about getting a pet, I thought of that dog. We had two kids and we acquired an assortment of cats, but no dog.

Then one sunny winter day when the sky was brilliant Colorado blue, I picked up my children at the sitter, and I saw the dog—Saint Bernard markings, but a golden retriever build. My friend said, "She's a stray. Do you want her?" I took her home.

My husband recognized her as the dog I always wanted. I named her Autumn. To my disappointment, we found her owner. That night my daughter and I both had dreams that we got Autumn back. The next day, the owner called and said Autumn had run away again. We could have her if we could find her. We found her at my neighbor's house. We figured she was looking for us. We kept her original name, Amber, and she was a bright spot in our family for many years.

Sometimes, it seems, people and pets just belong together. God cares about us and about our pets. He is big enough to care about even the little things that matter to us.

Thank You, God, that You not only care about people,
but animals, too.

How's Winnie's Leg?

Rise up; this matter is in your hands.
We will support you, so take courage and do it.
EZRA 10:4 NIV

We have to respect the courage of an animal in pain. Dogs try to hide their pain because in the wild, any sign of weakness would make them easy prey. Owners must be sensitive to their pet's needs. Once a dog starts showing pain, it's the real thing.

Our golden retriever was favoring one hind leg over the other, limping and sitting around like she didn't want to move too much. It was time to go to the vet, whether Winnie wanted to or not.

The vet prescribed quiet rest and a painkiller. When she didn't improve, we went to a chiropractor, who gave her three therapy sessions. An X-ray showed a torn ligament in her left rear leg. The vet scheduled surgery. Our baby was brave. We let her know we were there for her. We took her home to recuperate, and she had trouble getting up while wearing the splint and heavy bandage. She looked at us with sad eyes, wagging her tail as if to say, "I'm trying."

After two weeks, the bandage came off. She could put weight on the leg but sometimes reverted to hopping on three legs and keeping the affected leg raised. She loved the attention when we asked, "How's Winnie's leg?" Our love healed her more than anything.

Lord, thank You for Your all-powerful love.

Love and Sacrifice

Serve one another humbly in love.
GALATIANS 5:13 NIV

My food monster Lab, Sam, suffered with bouts of gastritis that started with vomiting—usually in the middle of the night. Our carpet steamer paid for itself many times over.

After multiple vet visits, I began treating Sam myself. I fed him boiled chicken, rice, green beans, and pills, and eventually the sickness would pass. But it was a lot of extra work from the first signs of gut trouble. I would often grumble. . .*not again!* The timing was always bad for me. But it was never good for Sam, either.

When we love others, animal or human, it often requires a sacrifice of time, money, and sleep.

"Sometimes I'm tired by the end of the day," a friend recently shared. Her husband and teen are on a special diet.

"I don't feel like cooking three meals a day. But when you love someone, you sacrifice—I regularly remind myself of Romans 12:1. 'Therefore, I urge you brothers, in view of God's mercy, to offer your bodies as living sacrifices, holy and pleasing to God—this is your spiritual act of worship.'

"It's not human nature to deny ourselves, or to put others first. I find if I think about pleasing God, I can serve those around me better."

Lord, thank You for daily reminders that Your love was demonstrated by sacrifice. Grant me Your heart to serve those You have blessed me with in life.

Not Alone

*"She gave this name to the Lord who spoke to her:
"You are the God who sees me," for she said,
"I have now seen the One who sees me."*

Genesis 16:13 NIV

Tiffany was a miniature poodle. Fluffy and white with just a touch of red, she was absolutely precious. Smart and sassy, she was also absolutely precocious.

Tiffany was easy to train because she understood my commands. Some days it seemed she spoke English as well as I did. I could tell her to go find the remote control, and she'd find it, exactly where I'd left it on the bathroom counter. Or I'd throw two stuffed animals and tell her which one to bring back, and she'd bring the correct one every time.

She understood more than commands. She understood emotions. When I was sad, she'd cry with me, cuddling up and licking my tears. When I was frustrated, she'd put her paw on my arm as if to say, "Calm down. It will be all right."

Tiffany lived to a ripe old age, and she died a long time ago. I miss her. But I still have Someone who understands me. While God doesn't follow my commands—I'm supposed to follow His—He does help me when I ask for it. When I feel sad or lonely or discouraged, I feel His presence gently comforting me, encouraging me, reminding me that I'm not alone.

Dear Father, thank You for being there. Thank You for understanding me when it seems no one else does. Thank You for never leaving me alone.

Dogs on Deployment

Foxes have dens to live in, and birds have nests,
but the Son of Man has no place even to lay his head.
LUKE 9:58 NLT

Angela and her husband, Andrew, are reservists with the US Coast Guard and US Marine Corps. When their overseas deployment notices arrived, they had a problem. What could they do with their two dogs? Their friend Georgia stepped in.

Georgia decided her house and yard were big enough for two more dogs. Now she is generously housing and feeding two very active dogs. Skadi and Luna may feel they have been deployed, too. Though they're in no danger of enemy attack in a foreign country, all that's familiar has been stripped away.

People and animals often find themselves uprooted from those they know and places they've called home. One woman who had to move numerous times because of her husband's job said she got beyond weary of tearful separations. "I got so tired of saying 'goodbye' that I finally stopped saying 'hello.'" The Lord Jesus contrasted His own itinerant lifestyle with foxes and birds. He, too, was bereft of a place to call home.

You may be in a position like Skadi, Luna, or the heartbroken woman who stopped making friends. Ask the Lord to meet your need today. He knows what you're going through.

Lord, for those of us displaced by circumstances
or crises, please strengthen us in our solitary days.

Relaxing in His Presence

Truly my soul silently waits for God; from Him comes my salvation.
He only is my rock and my salvation; He is my defense;
I shall not be greatly moved.

PSALM 62:1–2 NKJV

Romeo is a people person. Our half shih tzu, half dachshund always wants to be with us and hates to be alone. While I'm home, he has to be in the same room as me. If we leave the house to run to the grocery store or to church, he'll go upstairs and hide under our bed. As soon as he hears the garage door, he'll rush downstairs and greet us with a squeal. Overcome with excitement, he runs, jumps, and rolls on the floor until we get down on the floor with him to let him lavish us with kisses and hugs.

He prefers my husband, Blaine, over me. When Blaine travels for business—sometimes for several days at a time—Romeo pouts. He'll climb to the top of the stairs, rest his chin just on the edge of the step, and sigh deeply. As soon as Blaine returns and he spends a few minutes lavishing him with affection, Romeo is content to lie down near him and rest peacefully.

Lord, I want to be more aware of You. I want to experience
Your love. Help me to let go of the worries of life
and rest in Your presence.

The Mower

Stay with me; do not fear. For he who seeks my life seeks your life, but with me you shall be safe."
1 SAMUEL 22:23 NKJV

Zoey has a boundary collar that we have to put on her to remind her to stay safely away from the road. When she's wearing this, we have to remember to take it off if we're going to leave the boundary for a car ride or walk. When she was young, my husband, Dave, let her ride on the platform of his commercial mower between his feet. She began to think of the mower like a magic carpet of sorts. It seemed to bring her out of the boundary quite supernaturally. Zoey seemed to think the mower was a transporter, so she tried to hop on whenever Dave set out to mow. Many passersby would see this and smile. A grown man and his dog mowing the grass together.

Zoey's trust and joy in this simple habit remind me of the desire we all have to be safe, to be carried without harm to the places we want to go with the people we want to be with.

Father, help me trust You today to take me safely to the places I should go, whether physically or in my heart. I need You.

Walk with the Boots of Faithfulness

Let not mercy and truth forsake you; bind them around
your neck, write them on the tablet of your heart.
PROVERBS 3:3 NKJV

Boots was a trusted adviser. He survived the consumption of an entire squirrel. He was hit by a van. He lived through the devious tricks of a growing boy. Did I mention he was mostly Chihuahua?

He lived to see the arrival and departure of many other house pets. He slept while political scandal and gas rationing showed up on the evening news with Walter Cronkite. He observed me from my earliest years and stuck around after I left home as an adult. He's the dog I always associate with childhood.

As quirky as Boots might have been, he was loyal and remained in our family his entire life. As faithful as he was, Boots can't compare to God, who was faithful before we were born and will be faithful long after we pass.

Loyalty is something God talked about a lot. His faithfulness is greater than the most faithful pet, spouse, or friend. It is God's example that allows us to identify those special people and animals that reflect God's faithfulness in big and small ways.

Dear God, You want me to have a clear view of faithfulness.
Maybe that's why You created dogs. There are few animals
as faithful. Help me learn to demonstrate the same
loyalty and commitment You have shown me.

Spoiled

The eternal God is your refuge,
and underneath are the everlasting arms.
DEUTERONOMY 33:27 NIV

There's nothing quite like the contentedness of a dog when he knows his master is pleased with him. This old collie still loves me, as long as I scratch his ears. . .and even when I don't.

A little attention goes a long way. Eventually, I stop scratching his ears, and he flops down, usually right by my chair or on my toes. But the look in his eyes and the smile on his face don't change.

In truth, he spoils me way more than I spoil him.

Are we like that with God, or do we need Him to be "scratching our ears" all the time? Are we less content with God than our dogs are with us? How annoyed do we get with Him if He doesn't seem to be paying attention to us? Do we trust that He is still with us, supporting us, through the long stretches when there are no visible signs of that support? Or can we rest in His love the way our dogs rest in ours?

Lord, give me a contentedness, a patience, and a love
for You that leads me to serve You way more
than I need You to serve me.

Shiver Me Timbers?

You have searched me, LORD, and you know me. You know when
I sit and when I rise; you perceive my thoughts from afar.
You discern my going out and my lying down; you are familiar
with all my ways. Before a word is on my tongue
you, LORD, know it completely.

PSALM 139:1–4 NIV

"Look at your poor puppy! She's shivering!" Jolene's guest
commented after noticing the lap-sized dog outside the sunroom
door.

It was chilly. Adobe's round eyes spoke volumes about her
discomfort. When Jolene's guest let the furry pet inside, the canine
made herself part of the agenda—and the appetizers.

Jolene fell for her pet's shivering act at first. The short-haired
dog convinced most she was suffering outside in the weather.

But one day, Adobe shook pitifully outside the French doors
during a meeting, hoping to enjoy more appetizers.

Jolene noted it was over 100 degrees on that July day. When
she gave the dog a hard look, Adobe stopped shivering.

God's omnipresence may seem as invasive as secret
surveillance in one's private life. We can't fool God. He lets us make
mistakes and experience the consequences. But He cocoons us in
love and helps us up every time we ask. His love is always there. It
never fails. It's unconditional. It's forever.

Lord, thank You for loving me even through the mistakes.
I ask that You guide me.

Getting Grandpa's Eye

The Lord appeared to us in the past, saying: "I have loved you with an everlasting love; I have drawn you with unfailing kindness."
JEREMIAH 31:3 NIV

Grace and Dave had no intention of leaving with a dog when they stopped at the animal shelter. They'd come to look at cats for their son Phil, who lived in the apartment above their home. The staff greeted the couple like old friends. Grace and Dave had adopted four dogs over the years and sent a check every Christmas to support the no-kill shelter.

"Goldie, our Lab, passed on," Grace informed the director. "We're waiting to get a new one until after our summer cruise. We don't want to put a new dog in a kennel."

"Good thinking." The director took the couple to a back office and showed them the cat book. While the couple perused the photos of cats available for adoption, a door opened from a nearby inspection room. A black Lab named Coco trotted out.

Dave looked up just as the dog came straight up to him and nuzzled his hand. Then Coco set her paw on his knee.

That dog chose the couple for her forever family. Phil looked after Coco while they went on their summer cruise. Coco and the cat get along just fine.

Lord, let us be open to the movement of Your Spirit as You draw us together and prompt us to move in a direction that is beneficial.

Lady

I was talking recently with my friend Angela. She and her husband had been heartbroken when their first son died unexpectedly. Angela told me that comfort came from an unexpected place. "My husband and I left everything—our town, our house, our rescue dogs. We were devastated. One day, I found a Craigslist ad for an 'aggressive, untrainable border collie/greyhound mix.' It tugged my heart, so I called. When I went to see the dog, she jumped right into my arms, like a baby. Her owner had named her Tootsie, but I changed it to Lady. She never gave me any problems at all, but she was terrified of my husband at first." Angela's eyes welled up, but she smiled. "I wouldn't be here if it wasn't for Lady. She gave me a reason to get up every morning. I had to walk her and feed her. She had problems, and so did I. Lady helped me through my grief."

There was an even happier ending in store for Angela and her husband. "A year ago, we had another son." Angela's joy radiated. "He has *the same birthmark in the same place* as our first son. . .and I see my first son in him every day."

Lord, I trust that you are with me in the darkest night when I feel lost and bewildered.

Mad Dog

*"Do not make friends with a hot-tempered person,
do not associate with one easily angered,
or you may learn their ways
and get yourself ensnared."*

PROVERBS 22:24–25 NIV

Charlie had been mistreated. He was angry, and he didn't trust
people. My dad thought that with some TLC, Charlie would make a
great dog. But for a while, I couldn't even go in my backyard for fear
Charlie would attack me. My dad worked with him, trying to teach
him to trust us.

One day a neighbor boy's ball went into our backyard, and the
boy climbed our fence to get it. Charlie bit the boy, and we had to
find a new home for our angry pet. I had mixed emotions; I finally
had a dog, and now I had to get rid of him. But Charlie wasn't a
suitable dog for a family with children.

Charlie had potential to be a loving pet for someone, but we
weren't the right owners for him. In the same way, God wants us to
reach out to others. But sometimes, we're not the right people to
help a person. When that happens, instead of writing them off, we
can pray for them, believing God has a good plan for their lives.

Dear Father, give me wisdom to know when to get involved
in someone's life, and when to pray for them from
a distance and trust You with the results.

Puttin' on the Dog

*So God created mankind in his own image, in the image
of God he created them; male and female he created them.*
GENESIS 1:27 NIV

Our friend Brian has a photo of his French mastiff. Chuck is almost
as big as a pony and eats enough for three smaller dogs. In the
picture Chuck has a large stick in his mouth trapped between his
formidable incisors. He looks like a vampire dog, were there such a
thing.

Then Brian heard on the radio that people and their pets start
looking alike. If that's so, Brian is in big trouble. And if he *drools*
like Chuck. . . ?

It used to be called "puttin' on the dog" when people dressed
to impress. But what made people unique at the beginning was
not any kind of clothing, but their creation in God's image. By the
next generation, however, sin had spoiled perfection. Seth bore the
likeness of his father, Adam (Genesis 5:3).

Both Genesis 9:6 and Romans 8:29 remind us that what
was lost in Eden wasn't lost completely or forever. For now we're
instructed to "clothe [ourselves] with the Lord Jesus Christ"
(Romans 13:14 NIV). But it gets even better. That Romans 8:29 verse
reads, "For those God foreknew he also predestined to be conformed
to the image of his son" (NIV).

That's better than "puttin' on the dog" any day!

**Praise to You, Father, for the family
resemblance we will one day have in Christ.**

From Sorrow to Joy

Those who go out weeping, carrying seed to sow,
will return with songs of joy, carrying sheaves with them.
PSALM 126:6 NIV

Kim struggled when her only child graduated from law school, got married, and moved away from home. What Kim felt should have been a wonderful season in her life turned to horrible grief. Only a month later, her companion of thirteen years, a beautiful Cocker spaniel named Sammy, died. She chose to have Sammy cremated and promised never to go through the heartbreak of losing a pet again.

In spite of her promise to herself, she occasionally visited a local animal shelter. Each time she visited, she had to sign in and provide her phone number.

One morning Kim decided to bury Sammy in her rose garden. As she went to place him in the ground, her phone rang. Gigi introduced herself and said she'd received a phone call about a wonderful Schnauzer, and despite knowing Kim said she didn't want another dog, she insisted Kim should see him.

At first, Kim resisted, but finally agreed to meet him. When she walked into the shelter, four young men brought him out to her and she burst into tears. She said, "That is my dog!" She and Charlie bonded instantly. God turned her sorrow into joy.

Lord, sometimes I want to protect my heart from hurt,
but that often means refusing to love. Give me the
strength to let down my guard and love freely!

A Ride in the Truck

That which we have seen and heard we declare to you,
that you also may have fellowship with us; and truly our
fellowship is with the Father and with His Son Jesus Christ.
And these things we write to you that your joy may be full.

1 JOHN 1:3–4 NKJV

Some would say Zoey is big boned. Sturdy. A slow mover. So when it's time to go over to the neighbor's pond to fish and Zoey wants to go along (which is always), it is no easy task lugging her into the truck. We hoist her up to the truck bed and open the rear window so we can talk to her. Holding on around the turns and bumpy spots, Zoey stands near the cab in the corner and puts one of her legs over the cargo bar. Even though she occasionally gets a worried look in her eyes, she's so happy to face into the wind and let it take her ears back. She is always overjoyed when we arrive at the pond. She stands near the tailgate with a *now help me down* look on her face, so we do.

When I think about Zoey's behavior, I can't help but think of how I, too, long to be with others. What a pleasure it is to spend time with the people I care about. Best of all, God is right there with me in every breeze and bumpy turn.

God, bless this day with the fellowship of others,
that I might be part of Your children being a blessing to others.

113

Through the Valley

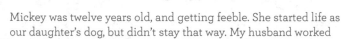

Mickey was twelve years old, and getting feeble. She started life as our daughter's dog, but didn't stay that way. My husband worked from home, and Mickey was his pal, happy to stay by his desk most of the time. They both enjoyed the close relationship.

One night she seemed to be failing rapidly, so we took her to an all-night vet, who wanted to keep her at the hospital for tests. We couldn't imagine her surviving the separation ordeal; she was too used to constant companionship. She seemed to understand that we wanted to keep her at home, and she even perked up a little.

The next day, our grandson and I were sitting on the family room floor, playing a game while Mickey was cocooned in one of her favorite places, behind the couch. We heard her snore occasionally, but then her breathing seemed to turn to gasps.

When we called, she dragged herself out, looked up at me, and laid her head on my lap. She took a deep breath. Then nothing. We tried everything we could think of to bring her back, but she was gone. She went very peacefully.

Were we right not leaving her with the vet? Definitely. She died in the comfort of her loving family.

**Lord Jesus, thank You for comforting us when
we grieve, and caring for our every need.**

The Cable Guy

*If you say, "The Lord is my refuge," and you make
the Most High your dwelling, no harm will overtake you,
no disaster will come near your tent.*

PSALM 91:9–10 NIV

Our most recent collie, Symba, was the happiest, most fun-loving dog I've ever known. *Everything* was a reason to have some fun. I get up. . .let's have fun. Someone new comes over. . .let's have some fun. Dinner's over. . .let's have some fun.

He was also very protective.

It happened with the cable guy. My wife was home alone when he arrived to install the system. Symba greeted him as he always does: "Let's have some fun!" After a while, however, my wife noticed that everywhere the cable guy went, Symba stayed between her and him. When he went into the basement, Symba parked himself at the top of the basement stairs. When he went to the second floor, Symba parked himself at the bottom of those stairs. Wherever the cable guy went on the first floor, Symba stayed halfway between. If they were facing each other talking, like when she paid the bill, Symba was sitting between. He was letting the guy scratch his head. He was happy. But he was between.

Never threatening, but always ready. My wife knew what would happen if the guy even thought about making an improper move.

**Lord, help me trust—simply trust—
in the protection of Your presence.**

115

A Mystery

*But each person is tempted when they are dragged away
by their own evil desire and enticed.*

JAMES 1:14 NIV

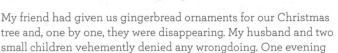

My friend had given us gingerbread ornaments for our Christmas tree and, one by one, they were disappearing. My husband and two small children vehemently denied any wrongdoing. One evening we all got into the car to go to a Christmas party, but I forgot something and went back into the house.

I walked in on our Saint Bernard/golden retriever mix, Amber, right in the middle of snatching a gingerbread ornament off the tree. "Aha!" She looked at me guiltily, gulped down the cookie, and trotted off to the hallway. Mystery solved. Amber clearly knew what she was doing was wrong. She had wasted no time to get her prize after she thought we were gone.

We are that way with God, aren't we? When we are feeling far from Him and unnoticed by Him, we are drawn to those things of instant gratification. We forget the facts. God is always near, and He loves us. Let's remember that though we may not feel His presence, He is with us. In the Lord's Prayer, Jesus taught His disciples to pray, "Lead us not into temptation" (Matthew 6:13 NIV). We'd do well to pray likewise.

**Father, thank You for always being near.
Help me remember that and do the things that please You.**

Love Is in a Name

He determines the number of the stars
and calls them each by name.
PSALM 147:4 NIV

When Grandma came to visit Fletcher's family, she entered the house with a suitcase in one hand and a flyswatter in the other. Fletcher cowered as he sought a place where he could hide from the flyswatter and her harsh words, "Dog, get off the sofa!" During her stay, he had been demoted to no-name "dog."

Grandma had lived on a farm. Each animal had a job to do. Dogs helped herd the livestock. None lived in the house.

When the stern woman left, Fletcher ambled through every room in the house. He gingerly lifted himself to the sofa and sighed. Once again, Fletcher was loved and was called by name—as we are.

What if God were as harsh as Grandma, waiting to punish those who get outside His favor and demoting us to beings without names? Who needs a flyswatter God?

All our lives, God calls us by name and beckons us to follow Him. He knows our lives and hearts long before our birth. Zechariah was to name his son "John." God sent His messenger to Mary to tell her that her son would be called "Jesus."

Be encouraged to know that you are special in God's thoughts, and He will give you His attention, care, answers to prayers, and gentle guidance.

Lord, help me to remember Your love
and name for me each day.

Mamzelle on Parade

Wisdom and money can get you almost anything,
but only wisdom can save your life.
ECCLESIASTES 7:12 NLT

William is a young tech professional with a bichon frise. Mamzelle is sweet and playful but also high maintenance. Her breed must be washed and groomed monthly or her white hair will mat.

William doesn't mind; he grooms Mamzelle at home. He has the time, being unemployed, so he studied tutorials, asked questions, and carefully practiced his clipping techniques. "She looks as good as when I took her to an expensive groomer. I love her to tears and won't trust her to anybody else."

William had three brothers growing up. To save money, their dad bought a grooming kit and learned to cut the boys' hair himself.

"It was good enough for me," William says, "and it works fine for Mamzelle. I clip her at our special grooming station I set up in the laundry room. I call it my Bella Boutique. Because she looks real *bella*, beautiful, when we're done."

His girlfriend, Amber, puts a bow in Mamzelle's hair and William's takes his two girls out for a walk. "Mamzelle thrives on the attention," Amber says, "and Will uses it to talk to people along the business district. He tells them he's looking for computer work and asks them for job leads."

Let us learn to be good stewards of our money and put our time to good use, so that we may prosper in life for the Lord.

Blessed are the Flexible

When I was single, both dogs slept on my bed on their blankets. At 120 pounds, my yellow Lab, Sam, took up half of the queen bed. He snored and jerked in his dreams, occasionally stunning me with a sudden slam roll.

Little Benji, weighing in at fifteen pounds, vigorously kneaded his pillow and smoothed all the wrinkles, then snoozed all night coiled up like a potato bug at my feet.

Sam would wake us both early barking for his food. It was annoying, but I loved being with them.

Then I met Steve and fell in love. He happens to be six-foot-three. Concerned, he wisely prepared all of us prior to the wedding. "The dogs can't sleep on our bed when we get married."

"Not even Benji?" I struggled as I reluctantly began to train the dogs to sleep on the floor four months before our marriage.

Then I recalled a conversation with a man in an auto-body waiting room.

"My wife is a veterinarian. We had two German shepherds sleeping on our bed when we first married." He laughed. "Now, we have four and upgraded to a king bed. Still, it gets pretty crowded."

It seems we all have to make adjustments in our marriages—one way or another.

**Help me be considerate of reasonable requests, Lord.
Keep me flexible so I won't be bent out of shape.**

Follow the Leader

"Come, follow me," Jesus said.
MATTHEW 4:19 NIV

As my husband and I sat in the car waiting for our thirteen-year-old son, we noticed a lady walking her dog. Only, she wasn't really walking her dog. The dog was walking her.

The dog, which looked to be a forty-pound German shepherd, pulled the woman this way and that, at times forcing her off the sidewalk, into a jog, even in circles around a tree. Those two provided some great entertainment while we waited. For some reason, though, I don't think the woman was nearly as entertained as we were.

All too often, I want to be like that dog, leading my Master around instead of following His lead. I appreciate the good things He does for me, but I don't want to submit to His will for my life. I have my own ideas, and I don't want to change my plans. I'd love for Him to come along, as long as He doesn't make me alter my course.

God doesn't work that way. He beckons us to "Come, follow Me." When we submit to Him, He will bless us. He'll protect us. He'll lead us on exciting adventures and give us peace for the journey. But He won't change his plans.

He won't force us into submission; we have free will. But if we want the pleasure of His presence in our lives, we've got to follow Him.

**Dear Father, help me to let go of my stubborn will.
I want to follow You.**

A Double-Dog Dare?

God cannot be tempted by evil, nor does he tempt anyone.
JAMES 1:13 NIV

A blend of Great Dane and Saint Bernard, Myles can easily remove food from almost anywhere he pleases. He sports a doleful look when Jacob or the rest of the family eats popcorn, but he never begs or snatches food. Well, almost never.

Myles doesn't take kindly to being left home alone. Twice the family came home to find the full flour canister sitting not on the counter, but on the living room carpet. The lid, complete with teeth marks, was off. No flour was spilled, and none dusted Myles's whiskers. The canister remained upright, as full as when the family left. How (or why) Myles did it remains a mystery. No one has dared him to repeat it; the canister gets put away now before Myles is left alone.

"If God exists, I dare Him to. . . ." The ellipsis can be filled in with any number of boasts. The first rule maker doesn't play by man's rules, however, and "does whatever pleases him" (Psalm 115:3 NIV). Our mighty God is so "other" that He doesn't indulge in "calling someone's bluff" or "getting even." Abraham's rhetorical question was, "Will not the Judge of all the earth do right?" (Genesis 18:25 NIV). He will, and He does. Every time, all the time.

Lord God, You alone are the great King.
Help me, Holy Spirit, to submit to the Father daily.

The Importance of Preparation

*But in your hearts revere Christ as Lord. Always be prepared
to give an answer to everyone who asks you to give the reason
for the hope that you have. But do this with gentleness and respect.*

1 PETER 3:15 NIV

Dee prepared for a trip home to see her parents. She was trying not
to worry about how her mother's boxer, Sadie, would react to Dee's
new Chihuahua, Daisy. Sadie had a reputation. She was infamous
for chasing the squirrels, and Dee and her mother were both afraid
she might mistake Daisy for a squirrel.

Dee's mom decided to do her best to prepare Sadie for Daisy's
visit. Unknown to Dee, her mom would speak to Sadie and say, "Dee
is bringing Daisy for a visit. She is a Chihuahua—not a squirrel—and
you can't chase her."

When Dee arrived, Sadie greeted her at the door. Dee sat down
and held Daisy in her lap for Sadie to see. Dee said, "Sadie, this is
Daisy; she's my baby. She's not a squirrel, so I don't want you to
chase her, okay?" The two became fast friends. During that visit
Sadie would stretch out in the sun in front of the window, and Daisy
would climb right up on her to sleep. Sadie became her favorite
sleeping spot.

**Heavenly Father, teach me to prepare my heart that I may know
how to respond to others in a way that points them to You!**

The Ladies

Let love be without hypocrisy. Abhor what is evil. Cling to what is good. Be kindly affectionate to one another with brotherly love, in honor giving preference to one another.
ROMANS 12:9–10 NKJV

Ever since our son Wes moved out west with his dog, Frank, Zoey is the only dog at our house. The first few weeks she was noticeably sad, but began to adjust with affection from others. She didn't seem to want to admit it at first, but she has befriended the cats, especially Eva. They are the only ladies in the household animal population. I often find them lying back to back in a patch of sun on the floor or in front of the fireplace to stay warm in the wintertime. The first few times we caught them together, Zoey would get up and move away as if nothing happened. Now she lets Eva love on her and looks up at me, like *Did you need something?*

It reminds me of how faithful God is to bring up just the companionship we need right when we need it. If He does this for me, why wouldn't He care about the animals in this way, too?

———————————————————————————

Lord, thank You for Your faithfulness to bring others alongside us, whether it's back to back or side by side, You are good.

Dot's Dash

Make your light shine, so that others will see the good
that you do and will praise your Father in heaven.
MATTHEW 5:16 CEV

If her mother hadn't been rescued, Dot wouldn't have lived to impact Andy, Kim, and all who met her. She was born in the garage, and was the runt of the litter. Her growth was impressive. She ultimately bore a resemblance to a jet-black greyhound.

She grew to become a companion, running buddy, and bunny patrol volunteer. She rode shotgun on Andy's weekend doughnut runs. Her rolling growl of affection was endearing.

She readily accepted my family when we visited. We'd held this giant of a dog when she was a pup. When we left last Christmas we had no idea she had only hours to live. She never let on she had cancer. She is missed.

Dot provides a picture of the impact we should make on the culture around us. God rescues us and then invites us to impact the world. We were never rescued just to sit silently, or even worse to make life miserable for others. We're encouraged to live in such a way that when we finish our lives, people will remember the God they saw us serve.

Dear God, You want me to represent You well. May what I say, think about, and do line up with Your plan for my life and the impact You want to make on those who know me.

Naps

The older I get, the more I think my collie has the right idea when it comes to naps.

The dog says, "What am I going to do for the next hour? Nothing!" More and more often, I agree.

The best thing is when the collie jumps up in the bed and naps with me, and when I wake up he's still there snoozing, curled at my feet or right up against my ribs. Sometimes I think God's a little like that with us. When we get the rest we need—whether it's on a Sunday or during a nap or a week's vacation away from our daily responsibilities—He rests with us. And like my collie, when I get up from my rest, God gets up from His rest, ready for some fun; ready for what *God* considers fun.

Sometimes I think the Sabbath was made to keep masters at home with their dogs. I know my collie thinks that!

When I need rest, I try to get it, and my collie has taught me not to be any more ashamed of it than he is.

**Lord, help me to slow down.
Help me to get rest when I need it.**

Getting the Suitcase Out

"Go in peace," the priest replied.
"For the LORD is watching over your journey."
JUDGES 18:6 NLT

Our English bulldog, Harvey, knew that whenever I pulled my travel case out of the closet, Mommy was going on a trip. He'd look at me with one dark eye appearing bigger than the other, almost like he was arching his eyebrow at me. That was his "Harvey" stare that pierced right into my soul.

You can't do this to me, Mom, said the look on his face. *I'm the best boy in the whole world.*

"Everything's going to be fine," I'd say to him. "Daddy will stay with Harvey. Daddy loves Harvey." I swear he knew what I meant by the comforting tone of my voice. My husband backed me up by showing extra loving attention to our doggie, trying to reassure him.

But he's not Mommy, our beloved boy seemed to project to us. Then he'd turn his back on us, lie down, and sulk. In the morning, I'd find one of my slippers gone. That meant he wanted to play our little game where I'd lament my lost slipper and he'd find it for me and bring it back. "You're my hero," I'd tell him with a hug. I always made sure to give him quality time before the van came to pick me up for the airport.

**Let us commit our journeys to the Lord, asking for traveling
mercies on the road and God's protection for
our loved ones left at home.**

False Bravado

If God is for us, who can be against us?
ROMANS 8:31 NIV

Dee's eyes danced as she recalled the day she drove through Lamar Valley in Yellowstone National Park with her dachshunds, Mulligan and Frankie, searching for wildlife.

"I couldn't believe my eyes! My little scouts barked in synchrony as we all peered out the passenger window. Two gray wolves circled in the meadow. I stopped the car and watched, mesmerized. Time passed until something caught my attention. I turned my head to look through the driver's window. Mulligan turned to bark but was stunned to silence. We stared at the belly of a grizzly bear standing straight up! He left scratches on my door as I peeled away, rejoicing in the blessing of seeing God's creatures in their natural environment."

Have you ever felt strong and in control, like Mulligan challenging wolves in a field where he was at a safe distance? Then the next moment, you're facing a giant right in front of you and reality hits you between the eyes. Intimidation soars—and the bravado flies out the window.

It's easy to boast when we are insulated from fear, but when we are confronted with potential danger, we need to trust in someone bigger and more powerful than us, who can take control of the driver's wheel and deliver us from evil.

Dear Lord, help me to trust You to navigate me into and out of adventurous and even perilous situations in this journey of life—no matter how prepared I feel in the situation.

127

Special

*I praise you because I am fearfully and wonderfully made;
your works are wonderful, I know that full well.*

PSALM 139:14 NIV

Every morning I walk with a friend at our local park. We're not the only ones walking; many dog owners are out at the same time, walking their dogs along the winding trails. I'm amazed at how many different types of dogs are represented there: Yorkies, Scotties, poodles, Labs, and mixes of every imaginable breed.

One thing they all seem to have in common, though, is they each have a master who thinks the world of them. These owners take the time each morning to load their dogs in their cars, drive to the park, attach a leash, and take them on a walk so they can get some exercise and share some quality time.

It's a good analogy for God's love for His children. Each one of us is unique. Some are tall and lean, others are short and stubby. . .but God thinks we're all adorable. Some of us have extreme gifts and talents, others are average, but God thinks each of us is extraordinary. He loves us passionately, and longs to spend time with us. And He goes to great lengths to make sure we have what we need, and to encourage a close relationship with Him.

I'm so glad I have a Master who loves me and thinks I'm special, just the way I am.

_____

**Dear Father, thank You for creating me, for loving me,
and for believing good things about me.
I want to be close to You.**

Not the Way of It

He has also set eternity in the human heart.
ECCLESIASTES 3:11 NIV

Death. We can dress it up, make light of it, or even try to ignore it. But it comes to all of us in one form or another, and it is always painful.

To my knowledge, Kristin had never cried over any pet. She and her family have had a number of pets through the years. Yet when I called her on a Saturday morning not long ago, her first words to me in a voice choked with tears were, "We had to put Lucy down this morning."

I cried right along with her.

At fourteen, their big, lovable black Labrador, Lucy, knew us almost as well as her family. She could still be as playful as a pup, though her movements had slowed and her breathing was labored. Kristin and her husband knew the time had come to put Lucy down. *Knowing* it made it no easier.

In those few words above from Solomon's pen we're reminded that death is not the way it was supposed to be. Sin came in accompanied by death, its inseparable partner.

Jesus Christ has broken the power of sin and death. (See 1 Corinthians 15:55–57.) We may yet die physically, but the eternity God set in our hearts will triumph because of our Savior.

**Lord, You know my pain in the loss of those dear to me.
Please comfort me as only You can.**

Laughter Lightens Your Load

We were filled with laughter, and we sang for joy. And the other nations said, "What amazing things the LORD has done for them."
PSALM 126:2 NLT

There were many concerns weighing heavily on Heather's mind as she and her husband, Michael, prepared to move from the Midwest to the Arizona desert. She wasn't sure how their two-year-old dachshund, Mattie, would handle the move. The second week in their new home, she and Michael sat down on the patio by the pool to relax. As they talked, their little dog began to run circles around the pool. Suddenly, Mattie miscalculated the corner turn and fell into the water. Michael tried to catch her, but he leaned in too far— he and the chair went in after her. Mattie seemed a little shocked, but she was okay.

Holding Mattie safely in his arms, Michael looked at Heather. Suddenly and unexpectedly, they both erupted into several minutes of uncontrollable laughter.

"Guess we've been taking life just a little too serious," Heather said, catching her breath. Michael agreed. "It sure felt good to laugh. I feel like a big weight was lifted."

Lord, when I worry and let anxiety in, remind me that my future is in Your hands. Give me a gentle tickle, so I'll make time to relax and have a good belly laugh.

Neighborhood Wandering

A new commandment I give to you, that you love one another;
as I have loved you, that you also love one another.
By this all will know that you are My disciples,
if you have love for one another."

JOHN 13:34–35 NKJV

On Facebook one evening I saw a photo of our dog with our young
next-door neighbor. The caption read "When Dave and Shelley are
away, Char and Zoey will play." It was so funny to see the secret
life of Zoey revealed on social media. She does like to disappear,
slipping away mysteriously at times, and now I know why. Who
could blame her? Char likes to play with her. I've learned that they
run around together, playing a version of tag. On this particular day
Char was playing a game of rocks with Zoey, apparently sharing
her most recent collection with her captive audience of one in
the backyard. In the photo, Zoey was loving Char's attention. It
was such a sweet image of reciprocal love, even if it was a toddler
playing with rocks and a dog who wanted to be petted.

Father, thank You for the people and pets You put in my life.
Grant me the willingness and grace today to
bless them as much as I am blessed.

My Friend Rudy

Put up with each other, and forgive anyone
who does you wrong, just as Christ has forgiven you.
COLOSSIANS 3:13 CEV

I never owned a dog with a more calming influence than Rudy. A small dog of unknown pedigree, Rudy was my answer to stress relief. No matter what my day was like, Rudy's gentle greeting helped change my attitude.

Rudy never bothered guests, quickly obeyed my commands, and was willing to spend as much time with me as I wanted.

She didn't mind her home-crafted haircuts. They never looked the same twice, but she never seemed to change her opinion of me, even when she was having a bad hair month.

We all need human friends like Rudy. People who stick around when it's easier to walk away. People who know our current stupidity is not a true indication of who God made us to be. People who still love us even when our actions give them a reason not to.

This is how God commands those who follow Him to act to toward each other.

Dear God, You want me to put up with people who irritate me, just like they have to put up with me. You gave me a perfect example in Jesus. When I can be patient with others, it shows those around me that there is a difference in me. The reason for that difference is You.

Accusations

He will not constantly accuse us,
nor remain angry forever.
PSALM 103:9 NLT

Mannix gave us a lot of laughs—and challenges. He was a cockapoo, the son of our cocker spaniel and a neighbor's poodle. If we didn't keep his hair trimmed, he looked like an unruly mop.

His first winter, he learned that in spite of his thick coat, if he shivered and looked pathetic, someone would let him back inside immediately. When he tried the same ploy in the heat of summer, he didn't seem to understand why we accused him of being a phony.

One December, something about the gift tags on our packages was irresistible to him. We found him under the tree repeatedly, chewing up tags. A few days before Christmas, I was in the kitchen and heard a strange swish, rattle, jingle, and plop from the living room. I ran to check, and there was the tree, stretched across the floor. "Mannix! Bad dog!" Before I had a chance to search for him, I remembered I had let him outside a few minutes earlier. He never realized I falsely accused him. We stood the tree back up and I put different tags on all the gifts.

Within a few days, he'd devoured a partial box of candy, chewed up a new toy, and pulled a gift sweater into his bed. But we couldn't not love him!

Heavenly Father, thank You for mercy we don't deserve.
Help us continually show Your heart to others.

133

Jealous

Kiss the Son, lest he be angry.

PSALM 2:12 KJV

Symba, our seventy-five-pound collie, had the weirdest habit. He wouldn't allow my wife and me to embrace.

If he even thought we were going to hug, he started moving between us. He liked me, but he loved and protected her. When we would hug—and sometimes we did it just to get his reaction—he would try to work his snout and his body between us. If that didn't work, he'd start barking: first a muffled whimper, then a whine, then a full-fledged bouncing bark.

What calmed him down? If either of us bent down and hugged *his* neck.

He was protective of her, but he couldn't bring himself to attack me. I think he was also very, very jealous of the attention he wasn't getting.

God says that He is like that. "For I, the LORD your God, am a jealous God" (Exodus 20:5 NIV). God can stand us paying attention to a lot of things; He can't stand us *embracing* anything but Himself.

He'll register His disapproval until we return to embracing Him. It's for our own good.

Father, show us when we're giving anything but You our complete attention. Return us to Yourself, and when we embrace You again, embrace us back.

Glory and the Rattlesnake

Cast all your anxiety on him because he cares for you.
1 PETER 5:7 NIV

One day my friend Kathie noticed the beautiful plumed tail of her Australian shepherd, Glory, was drooping. She wondered if her other dog, Keesha, had jumped on her too hard and hurt her back. Kathie took Glory to the vet, who noticed a bump on the dog's hip. He shaved it to reveal two puncture marks. The vet said, "Your dog has been bitten by a rattler." Glory narrowly escaped death.

Rattlesnakes, car accidents, home invasions—with so many bad things out there, it's a wonder that anyone makes it through a day alive, yet we do. The Bible tells us about angels who intervene and protect people. "Are not all angels ministering spirits sent to serve those who will inherit salvation?" (Hebrews 1:14 NIV). Jesus said that a sparrow doesn't fall without God knowing and we are more important than the sparrows (Matthew 10:31).

With all of the death, disease, and destruction in the world, it's easy to become frightened. Let's take heart and be brave, knowing that God provides for and protects all of His children. When bad things do happen, for one reason or another, God will work in it for our good (Romans 8:28).

Father, thank You for watching over me and meeting my needs. I pray that all I think, say, and do will be to Your glory.

Full of Life and Sandwiches

The thief comes only to steal and kill and destroy;
I have come that they may have life, and have it to the full.
JOHN 10:10 NIV

While Jeannie had her pint-sized sons, Rob and Rick, help pack for the picnic and hike, four-year-old Rob wanted to know if they could take their dog, Frosty. Jeannie thought this was a great idea.

Right after lunch, they would be following a canyon trail, so Jeannie didn't bring a table. At the trailhead, she spread out a tarp topped with a tablecloth. She seated her sons and passed a sandwich to each. Frosty nuzzled close to Rob at eye level. Though she didn't eat from the table at home, Frosty turned her mouth just so. As the boy bit down on one end of his sandwich, Rob turned to see the pet had chomped the other end. "It's okay, Frosty," he whispered. "You need trail food, too."

More than our need for trail food, we need confidence in the foundation of faith from God's promises. The thief whispers, "You can't do it." God counters, "You can, and I'll help you." The thief proclaims, "This is all there is." God responds, "Your abundant life starts now to forever."

Abundant life builds in faith, memories, experiences, and time with God and others—from here to eternity.

Lord, nudge me to counter the negative with Your words and remember moments of Your abundance.

The Dog Is Slowing Down

I will be your God throughout your lifetime—until your hair is white with age. I made you, and I will care for you. I will carry you along and save you.

ISAIAH 46:4 NLT

Uncle Jay, age eighty-nine, came to live with his niece and her family just when their Dalmatian, Delmer, was getting old. "Unc" was widowed and recovering from surgery. Ten-year-old Delmer was less active than in his younger days. The dog preferred lounging on the rug to running after a ball. The kids didn't find their pet as exciting as before.

The animal was lonely.

Unc, however, quickly bonded with "old boy" Delmer. "We've got something in common. We're both senior citizens," Unc said, laughing. "The dog moves slow. I take the steps slow."

Both his doctor and the dog's vet prescribed the same thing for their patients. Light exercise. Lose weight. Eat healthier. The two took gentle walks around the yard together. The dog sat at Unc's feet while Unc surfed online for medical news. He found helpful suggestions to give to his new family.

"You shouldn't feed the dog cookies. They're not good for him. I cut back on sugary treats to take weight off my joints. Dogs have the same issue."

Unc's research helped keep both the dog and his niece's family healthy. Their time together was beneficial and happy for all.

Thank You, gracious God, for giving us companions along life's way. May we be faithful to share our love and encouragement with others.

Apologize

And do not grieve the Holy Spirit of God.
EPHESIANS 4:30 NIV

Donna grimaced as she remembered a recent experience with her Italian greyhound. "I was recovering from an injured disc in my neck, and Sammie kept nuzzling my arm. The pain was unbearable—I just couldn't handle being touched. The nerve pain shot from my neck down my arm whenever Sammie nudged me. I snapped. I swatted him on the nose, and he cowered away. I had never been so harsh with him." Donna shook her head.

"When I was driving later that night, the song 'Mandy' was on the radio. Did you know Barry Manilow wrote that song about his dog? I substituted Sammie's name in the lyrics—'Sammie, you came and you gave without taking and I turned you away.' Suddenly, I started bawling. When I got home, I was still sobbing when I found Sammie and hugged him. I told him I was sorry for pushing him away when he was just trying to comfort me. I knew he could tell I wasn't feeling well and just wanted to help. He loved the attention! He was licking the tears right off my face."

How many times have we felt guilty because we know we have been short with people we love—a spouse, a parent, a child—and just expect them to understand without explanation or remorse?

Lord, help me to be humble and sensitive to Your Spirit's
prompts to apologize to anyone I have hurt.
May I see their feelings beyond my own.

138

Natural Instinct

You were taught, with regard to your former way of life,
to put off your old self, which is being corrupted by its deceitful
desires; to be made new in the attitude of your minds;
and to put on the new self, created to be like God
in true righteousness and holiness.

EPHESIANS 4:22–24 NIV

We live in the country, and we have ducks and chickens. We keep a scrap bucket by the sink, and each day we give the scraps to our birds. Ginger, our basset hound (who, by the way, gets plenty of treats of her own), doesn't think this is fair.

She thinks all treats should belong to her. Given the chance, she'll push her way into the chicken pen and gobble up the leftover corn or rolls or whatever else we had for dinner. She's only doing what comes naturally to her; her instinct is to want good, yummy things.

By nature, humans are the same way. We clamor to get what we want. But Jesus showed us a different way. He wants us to become new creatures, created to be like God. He said to put others' needs and wants ahead of our own. He said if we want to be great, we must be servants. That goes against our natural instincts.

When we choose to follow His example, we may miss out on a few extra treats along the way. But when we follow Him, the rewards of living a service-filled life come back to us many times over.

Dear Father, help me to set aside my selfish desires.
I want to be like You.

Hero of the Year

The righteous are bold as a lion.
PROVERBS 28:1 KJV

Did you know there is a "Hero of the Year" award presented each year on National Dog Day? A young English cocker spaniel once won the award after the dramatic rescue she initiated.

Michael and Honey were involved in an automobile accident. After rolling into a ravine and landing upside down, Michael found himself badly injured and hanging by his seat belt. Unable to free himself, he gave a command to his dog of only a few weeks.

"Go get help, Honey."

Honey ran over a half mile to a farmhouse, where her barking alerted the home owner. She kept whimpering until the woman, telephone in hand, followed her back to the wrecked SUV. After the 911 call, and while paramedics extricated Michael, Honey paced back and forth nervously. The happy ending found Honey next to Michael numerous times during her master's hospitalization and recovery.

Most of us—and most of our dogs—will never get to play the part of a hero. But our Savior, Jesus Christ, is the superhero of all time and eternity. He went to the furthest extreme to save us. God the Son took on human form and flesh and died to save us from the sin from which self-extrication is impossible.

Looking for a hero? Look no further than Jesus, the One hailed as the triumphant "Lion of the tribe of Judah" (Revelation 5:5 NIV).

Lord Christ, You are my hero, and I praise You.

Obedience and Blessings

"Behold, I set before you today a blessing and a curse:
*the blessing, if you obey the commandments of the L*ORD *your*
God which I command you today; and the curse, if you do not obey
*the commandments of the L*ORD *your God, but turn aside from*
the way which I command you today, to go after
other gods which you have not known."
DEUTERONOMY 11:26–28 NKJV

Megan grew up with three incredible Rottweilers. She was thrilled
when her husband, Mike, came home with a Rottweiler puppy. They
named him Samson. With plans to start their family in a couple
of years, she knew Samson would be a wonderful family dog, but
she also knew that most Rottweilers could be a little stubborn and
needed a firm training hand from an experienced handler—which
Mike was not.

Mike enrolled Samson in obedience school. Mike quickly
learned that if Samson was given leadership of their family pack, he
would assume command, and Mike would lose all control. Samson
proved to be extremely smart. He bucked hard against Mike's
leadership at first. The trainer encouraged Mike and gave him
excellent advice.

After a few weeks, Meagan saw growth in both of them. She
was proud of them and realized the blessing Samson would be to
their future family.

Lord, thank You for Your leadership. Forgive me for when
I rebel and help me to understand that obedience in
following You brings blessings to my life and family.

Thunder

*The earth is the L*ORD*'s, and all its fullness, the world and those who dwell therein. For He has founded it upon the seas, and established it upon the waters.*

PSALM 24:1–2 NKJV

Before I even heard the thunder clap, our seventy-pound puppy, Frank, was jumping on my bed in the middle of the night whining in desperate need of comfort. Right behind him was his mama, Zoey, thankfully too large and uncoordinated to jump on the bed with him. This happened every time we had a thunderstorm. It could take hours to calm them down, especially Frank. We needed a sound-proof room without windows!

None of us can recall when it happened that Frank became deathly afraid of thunder and lightning. Zoey did not have this fear until Frank developed it. Somehow these mighty forces of God's green earth became Frank's foe.

I have to wonder how often I am like this. Sometimes I don't understand why something causes me to react in an extreme way. I'm complicated to be sure.

Lord, You work in the mightiness of the earth You created. Move in my heart in mighty ways, too. Show me the next part of my heart that needs healing.

A Privilege

*May the Lord make your love increase and overflow for each
other and for everyone else, just as ours does for you.*
1 THESSALONIANS 3:12 NIV

There's something about walking a slow, old dog in a forty-degree
rain shower at 3:15 a.m. that makes other things seem a little better.

How much are we willing to put up with for the sake of those
we love? You can smell that the baby needs changing; the wife is
snoring after a very long day. Grandpa's wandering again, and he
needs strong arms to get him back into the bed.

So when the old collie nuzzles you awake, apologetically, at
3:06 a.m. because he has to go out? It's not an aggravation.

It's an opportunity.

It's a privilege. Because it's when we serve that we begin to love
like our Lord loved. Service isn't service if there's nothing difficult
about it. Our faithfulness in the hard times feeds our joy in the good
times; it becomes much, much sweeter.

Lord, help me to wrap Your towel around my waist,
and wash the feet You call me to wash. You stooped for me.
Let me always be eager to bend down and lift those
near me who cannot lift themselves.

Glory and the Coyotes

Be alert and of sober mind. Your enemy the devil prowls
around like a roaring lion looking for someone to devour.
1 PETER: 5:8 NIV

One day when my friend Kathie was walking on her ranch, she looked up to see her dog, Glory, chasing a coyote. Immediately two other coyotes took off after them. She knew that coyotes used the old trick of one being bait, while the rest of the pack went in for the kill. She called Glory, who immediately returned to her mistress's side. Kathie was grateful for Glory's quick response.

In John 10, Jesus spoke of being the shepherd. He said that His sheep knew His voice and they wouldn't follow a stranger. Jesus also said, "I am the good shepherd. The good shepherd lays down his life for the sheep" (John 10:11). He did, indeed, lay His life down for His people.

Satan is like those hungry coyotes and wolves. What will save us from danger in this life is listening for, recognizing, and obeying the Lord's voice. Let's read God's Word, pray, and fellowship with other Christians so that we may be more sensitive to His Holy Spirit. Like Glory, let's be quick to respond to His call.

Lord, thank You for giving Your life for Your sheep.
Please help me be sensitive and obedient to Your
Spirit and respond quickly when You call.

Night Watchman

God will command his angels to protect you wherever you go.
PSALM 91:11 CEV

A low growl woke Mother near midnight.

"Toni?" she whispered. "What's wrong, girl?" With Daddy out of town, the vigilant collie served as our protector.

Toni poked Mother's arm with her cold nose and growled again, then crept toward the hallway. A gust of warm air lifted the bedroom curtains. Outside a twig snapped. Gravel crunched. Mother slid out of bed, grabbed the rifle hidden behind the door, and followed Toni to the living room. The collie stopped at the window, her fur rising.

Footsteps ascended the front porch. Mother aimed the rifle with trembling hands. My five-year-old brother, Jimmy, yelled from behind her, "Mommy, is the gun loaded?"

Footfalls pounded down the steps, scattering gravel. Mother called the police. The officers arrived within minutes and found a man's footprints leading from the bedroom window to the porch. When they came inside, Toni stood as sentry between them and her family.

One policeman held his hand out for Toni to sniff before petting her. "She's a great night watchman." Her wagging tail beat against Mother's legs. A patrol car remained by the curb for the rest of the night. Inside the house, Jimmy slept soundly next to Mother, with Toni at the foot of the bed, dozing with one ear cocked upward.

God enlists many of His creatures to watch over His people.

Thank You, Lord, for Your protection.

Quirks

Accept the one whose faith is weak,
without quarreling over disputable matters.
ROMANS 14:1 NIV

"What type of dogs are those?" I asked the woman next to me at the veterinarian office.

She dangled each leash. "This is a terrier mutt, a Maltese, and a pug." She leaned forward to pat the last dog. "This guy's the reason I'm here—he has dry eye."

Jet-black peepers bulged straight at me.

"Every morning we come in for his eye drops. My other pug at home needs eye drops every day, too, but this one is difficult." She shook her head. "As soon as I pick up the dropper, he growls. I can't get near him."

The vet assistant approached and kneeled before him. He wagged his stumpy tail and sat quietly as she placed his eye drops— then rewarded him with a treat.

"He loves to come here. He takes his drops and treats happy as a lark. I don't mind, though. We use this time for our morning walk." The owner smiled.

I'm not that patient when my dad makes repeat requests that involve a forty-five-minute drive. When he asked me to come help him empty the voice mail on his cell phone, I asked him to go to the store for help instead.

If I could learn to enjoy the drive past cows, sheep, and winding hills away from the urban sprawl, maybe helping my dad would become a blessing in disguise.

**Lord, help me not to criticize, but instead to walk
an extra mile of kindness for those I love.**

Rescuer

So do not fear, for I am with you; do not be dismayed,
for I am your God. I will strengthen you and help you;
I will uphold you with my righteous right hand.

ISAIAH 41:10 NIV

Jacobi was a black Lab. He was obedient and loyal, intelligent and alert. Because his owner's landlord didn't allow pets in the house, Jacobi spent his nights in a kennel in the backyard.

One night, a fierce storm caused flash flooding. In minutes, Jacobi's kennel was afloat. When Mark, his owner, rushed into the storm to rescue Jacobi, he found the dog paddling furiously, struggling to keep his head above water. Soon enough, Jacobi was safe inside the utility room, with warm towels and a space heater.

Sometimes it seems life's storms will take us under. We paddle furiously and struggle to keep our heads above water, and wonder if we'll be swept away at any moment. We need to keep paddling, but we can do so with confidence, knowing we have a rescuer. He's on his way, and though life may get hard at times, He won't let us drown. Soon, we'll find ourselves in the safety of His warm embrace.

Dear Father, I know You will never let me go through more
than I can handle. I know that if I just keep paddling,
just keep trusting You and believing in Your goodness,
You will rescue me. Please come soon, Lord,
for I need to be rescued.

The Un-Hero

Do not withhold good from those to whom it is due,
when it is in your power to act.
PROVERBS 3:27 NIV

Not long after Chris read the account of Honey, the Hero of the Year dog (see page 140), she gave her own blond cocker spaniel, Honey, a long look.

"Would you do the same for me, Honey?" Chris received a yawn in return.

Not many weeks later, Chris and Honey took their daily walk. The walk had been delayed until after dark. Nothing happened out of the ordinary until Honey saw a rabbit to their right. Her sudden, hard, sharp tug on the leash knocked Chris off balance. Chris went down hard on the concrete curb.

The rabbit disappeared and Honey stood looking dumbfounded at Chris. The cocker sat her doggie derriere down with another yawn, regarding Chris with little more than a bored curiosity. Any request from Chris for her Honey to go get help was futile. With a fractured hip, Chris had to pick herself up and walk home with her oblivious, not at all heroic dog.

"When he [Jesus] saw the crowds, he had compassion on them" (Matthew 9:36 NIV). Jesus never acted on impulse, but He never turned away from people, either.

That's how I want to live. Any given opportunity may not come with hero potential, but I want to walk in the Master's way.

Lord, give me Your sensitivity to others,
and help me to practice kindness daily.

Follow the Leader

By faith Abraham obeyed when he was called to go out
to the place which he would receive as an inheritance.
And he went out, not knowing where he was going.
HEBREWS 11:8 NKJV

Our small half shih tzu, half dachshund, Romeo, becomes so excited when I mention the word "walk." It's like telling a child you'll take him for ice cream. He runs to me and then from door to door, unsure which exit he should take.

We normally walk around our neighborhood, but I go in different directions just to keep it interesting. As we start out, Romeo normally leads the way, but after we cross a few streets, or I tug on his lead a little to let him know we aren't going the way he has his nose pointed, he follows closely behind me.

Are you that way with God? I know I am. God says, "We're going," and I normally am ready for the adventure. Sometimes I become overly confident in the directions, only to look back and realize I don't know where I'm going. Thankfully, all we have to do is look to Him for direction and follow His lead.

Lord, I am excited about my journey with You.
Forgive me when I try to lead or get ahead of You.
Thank You for keeping me safe and pointed
in the right direction.

Corn Culprit

When I kept silent, my bones grew old through my groaning
all the day long. For day and night Your hand was heavy
upon me; My vitality was turned into the drought of summer.
I acknowledged my sin to You, and my iniquity I have not hidden.

PSALM 32:3–5 NKJV

There was a scuffle on the front porch one night outside my window that I couldn't pinpoint. The next day, the decorative autumn Indian corn that was in a basket was now on the floor and missing a few kernels. I was sure it was raccoons. I knew they were crafty, due to the loss of our sweet corn in the backyard garden. It would be difficult to keep them from getting this corn, too. Sure enough, the next day I found the decorative corn down again with a few more kernels missing. A pattern. Darn those raccoons! Zoey came up to the porch to console me, and she cleaned up the kernels left behind. How sweet.

A couple days later I noticed the three-ear bundle of corn completely missing from the porch. With all its missing kernels it was much lighter to carry now and surely the scoundrel had run off with it. Then I saw Zoey lying out front under some trees with the bundle of corn, stripping off the kernels like a champ. Clearly this was not her first rodeo. Caught red-pawed, she looked up at me with confession in her eyes. What else could I give her but grace? Hey, it took her a while, but she was owning it.

Lord, help me to acknowledge my wrongdoing and confess my brokenness to You, so that I might move forward in the journey of redemption and freedom in You.

He Enjoyed Retirement

Oh, give thanks to the L<small>ORD</small>, for He is good!
For His mercy endures forever.
P<small>SALM</small> 136:1 NKJV

Scruffy came to live with us when he was two. He was housebroken, obedience trained, and he'd been a show dog. He was a registered schnauzer who'd never seen his reflection and had never been petted.

He was groomed for the show circuit, but at the age of two, Scruffy was past his prime. He enjoyed his fifteen years of retirement. He discovered joy in the human touch. While he was not a puppy when he met us, he acted like one the rest of his life.

I've never met a dog that responded so completely to love. He couldn't wait for us to get home, couldn't wait to nudge his nose under our hands to be petted, and couldn't stop showing gratitude. Scruffy acted like he was the most fortunate dog that ever walked the earth.

I wonder if God is delighted when we show as much gratitude as Scruffy. God rescued, forgave, and offered eternal life. Many will accept His rescue and gifts, but long-term gratitude is a little harder to come by. When we become who God made us to be, we can be grateful, because our lives *will* change.

Dear God, You want me to be grateful, to know that living for You is better than anything I've experienced, and to choose to rejoice because of Your great gifts. May the rest of my life be a living thank-You.

Limits

*If anyone comes to me and does not hate father and mother,
wife and children, brothers and sisters—yes, even their own
life—such a person cannot be my disciple.*

LUKE 14:26 NIV

Yes, a dog wants what he wants. Dogs are, as has often been observed, master manipulators (pun intended). But then he senses that you're sick, and flops his 102-degree body beside you in the bed or on the couch. Or he senses that you're angry, and he courageously comes in and looks at you with those sheepish, angelic, frightened eyes to calm you down. Or he comes between you and any possible danger.

What wouldn't he do for you? What wouldn't we do for God?

Where are the limits of our dogs' love for us? Where are the limits of our love for God?

God will find a way to find them out. When that happens, we'd better be as ready to show God that our love for Him is limitless, just as our dogs are to show us the same thing.

**Heavenly Father, Master of our souls, keep our hearts as ready
for the test as Your Son was for Gethsemane. Let our cry to
You be of love and of limitless dedication. Our dogs love
us to the death; Your Son loved us to the death.
Please, by Your Spirit, give us the same heart.**

Frolicking with the Enemy

You adulterous people, don't you know that friendship
with the world means enmity against God?
JAMES 4:4 NIV

My friend Kathie heard barking coming from the barn, where her two Anatolian shepherds, Malachi and Athena, faithfully guarded her alpacas. Kathie looked out her window, and saw Athena, her fun-loving guard dog, playing with a coyote. They stood on either side of the fence, Athena's tail wagging, and then both the coyote and Athena would get down on their front legs and playfully jump at each other. Kathie stepped out of the house and shouted, "Athena, you're supposed to be growling, not playing!" The coyote ran off.

The Bible says to do what's best for our human enemies. In doing so, we heap burning coals on their heads. But the enemy of our souls, Satan, we should resist. We become the enemy of God by taking in the ways of the secular world.

Unwittingly, we play with our spiritual enemy. This can be evident in the shows we watch and the clothes we wear. We fraternize with the enemy when we give in to the secular world, one attitude at a time. Let's rise up in fierce anger against those things that would damage our relationship with our Creator and ruin our lives.

Dear Lord, help me love the things You love and hate the things You hate, all the while treating our human enemies with kindness, trusting that You will bring their evil deeds to nothing.

A New Meaning for Lost and Found

There will be more rejoicing in heaven over one sinner
who repents than over ninety-nine righteous
persons who do not need to repent.

LUKE 15:7 NIV

"I guess that's about it," Jamey called to the three teens seated inside the SUV as she fastened a leash on their hound, Maxine, to lead her to the vehicle. "We're packed up. Boys, we're ready to go home!"

But Maxine's nose beckoned her to the fascinating smells in the forest. The ham-sized dog twisted out of her harness and sprinted into the thick underbrush.

"Oh no! This is bear country! Go get her!"

Though the four called and searched, Maxine was gone.

"What should we do now, Mom?"

"We'll just wait for a while. If she doesn't come back, we'll go."

After nearly an hour, Maxine came trotting back as if to say, "Wow! I wouldn't have missed that smell for anything!"

God is patient. There are times when we run away from God or feel the irresistible pull of a trail diverted away from Him. That path might span hours, days, years, or decades. But God still waits for our return. When we come back, there is great rejoicing.

Lord, thank You for answered prayers, even when I must wait.

Welcome Home!

But when he was yet a great way off, his father saw him,
and had compassion, and ran, and fell on his neck, and kissed him.
LUKE 15:20 KJV

Babe, our one-year-old boxer, became an escape artist to rival
Houdini. In her zeal to greet me as I walked home from my fifth
grade class, she broke two collars and three small chains.

Attaching her leash to a stake in the ground proved worthless.
Babe dragged the stake behind her as she ran to me through the
vacant lot behind our house.

My father decided to create a stronger barrier to keep her
restrained. He built a six-foot-high fence around the backyard.
Filling a trench with cement along the perimeter thwarted her
efforts of digging an escape tunnel.

As I approached the house with my friends, Babe soared
over the fence like a superhero. She bounded across the vacant
lot toward me. I braced for her catcher's mitt paws to hit me in the
chest and knock me down. She plastered my face with doggy kisses.

I had been at school only a few hours, and yet Babe launched
herself over a high hurdle to welcome me home. Like the prodigal
son's father, she waited with hope for my return.

Heavenly Father, thank You for Your mercy. When we leave
Your protection, You watch for us, ready to welcome
us home with love and compassion as we
return to the shelter of Your loving arms.

Morning by Morning

He wakens me morning by morning,
wakens my ear to listen like one being instructed.
ISAIAH 50:4 NIV

My friend Valerie was telling me about her dog, Bella, who loves their morning routine.

"Every morning Bella rises with me. She sits up as I begin to stretch my legs in bed. When I say, 'Time to get up,' she jumps down, tail wagging, and tromps to the kitchen to 'get some sips' of water. She doesn't understand why my 'sips' of coffee take longer. When I tell her, 'Time to get ready,' she knows to lie on the tub mat while I get ready for work. When I say, 'Time for Bible study,' she knows the most important part of our routine is about to begin." Valerie smiled as she told me this.

"Bella lies at my feet quietly while I read the Word of God and pray. Sometimes she presses her paw against my leg while I'm praising God, which is so soothing. When I pat her head reassuringly, she seems as comforted by me as I am by my Master. Every dog trainer and training book I've referenced told me dogs need a master who is in charge, or they will basically run wild. Our routine, with all its habits and boundaries, creates something for Bella to look forward to, while also giving her stability. My daily routine of reading God's Word and expressing my gratitude brings me peace I can't do without. I think Bella would agree."

Lord, help me to daily still myself before You and read Your Word, so I can receive Your instruction, comfort, and wisdom.

Staying Connected

*Therefore encourage one another and build up
one another, just as you also are doing.*
1 THESSALONIANS 5:11 NASB

Shamgar liked to watch television, especially if there were dogs in the show. Whenever he heard a canine bark or growl from the screen, or even saw another dog on television, he'd sit as close as possible and stare, transfixed. He enjoyed seeing other dogs. I guess it made him feel like he wasn't alone.

He also went crazy when he heard another dog pass by in the street. If a neighbor's dog barked, he'd bark back in an exclusive, just-for-dogs conversation. It was important for him to feel connected to other dogs.

It's important for us to connect with other Christians. We need that camaraderie with like-minded people to remind us we're not alone. It's easy to get so busy going to work, running errands, and living life that we forget to make time for friendships with those who believe as we do. Those friendships are a lifeline for us when life gets stormy. Those relationships are a comfort to us when we're sad. Those are the people who encourage us when we're ready to give up. When we make time to stay connected to other Christians, it reminds us that we're not alone in this journey called life.

Dear Father, thank You for the gift of friendship. Help me to make time to nourish the friendships I have, and to reach out to others who may not have as many friends as they need.

Like My Looks?

People look at the outward appearance,
but the LORD looks at the heart.

1 SAMUEL 16:7 NIV

It had been a long three years for Sharon and her "untrainable" dog, Sparky.

This little dachshund/Doberman mix, who is a rescue dog, has suffered from separation anxiety since Day One. He's smart and lovable, but he does not like being alone. He chewed his way out of his cage. Another time he chewed his way out of the house!

Fortunately, Sparky has learned that when his people leave, they always return. Sharon remembers why she picked out Sparky: his prominent overbite. That charming facial flaw on Sparky's muzzle isn't quite so endearing after those costly home repairs.

Most of us see one thing (maybe more) about our bodies we would like to change. In the United States alone, more than ten billion dollars is spent annually on cosmetic surgery. Whether a less-than-perfect appearance endears us to another, or gives us private reason to pout, nothing in our physical looks rates importance with the Lord; He looks within.

What's within looks no better to the Lord than what, on the outside, may look bad to me. God goes about doing His own kind of surgery—not cosmetic surgery, but heart surgery. He calls it a "circumcision of the heart, by the Spirit" (Romans 2:29). Once the divine surgeon does His work, we are lookin' good—no matter what our outer appearance.

Lord, I pray to be wholeheartedly devoted to You.

Do It for Fun

God cares for you, so turn all your worries over to him.
1 PETER 5:7 CEV

"Rain or shine, sleet or snow, Arthur is all in," Jimmy yelled to his wife, Sharon, as he came back in from shoveling snow in the driveway. He stopped in the laundry room to dry off their six-year-old Shiba Inu's feet.

"He doesn't want to miss the fun," Sharon agreed.

"I just love him so much," Jimmy said. "He gets out there and has so much enthusiasm. His love for me and for the outdoors keeps me excited and makes my work go so much faster. I can't imagine having a bad attitude about shoveling snow or doing yard work when he's out there cheering me on."

"Yes, and when you look at him, he's always smiling and having a good time. He's a natural cheerleader. He doesn't have a care in the world as long as he's with us."

"Think about that for a second," Jimmy said. "He has nothing to worry about because he knows we'll take care of him. Imagine what we'd be like if we let go of all our cares and just trusted God in the same way Arthur trusts us."

Jesus, You came to give me an abundant life. Forgive me for trying to work things out on my own and help me to give my worries to You. You have promised to perfect what concerns me, and I trust You to do that.

Waddling Together

Lead me in Your truth and teach me, for You are the God of my salvation; on You I wait all the day. Remember, O LORD, Your tender mercies and Your lovingkindnesses, for they are from of old.
PSALM 25:5–6 NKJV

I like to walk or run along the river path next to our house in the country. The path is a family favorite that my sons keep mowed for all of us to enjoy. Sometimes Zoey will wander down the path on her own and take a walk. She usually whines to come with me when I head out on the path. I usually take her, but sometimes it's not easy with the pace she keeps. Most large country dogs are too fast to run with. Zoey on the other hand, waddles wherever she goes.

I often have to stop and wait for her to catch up, or call her when she wanders off toward a distraction. I try to remember that this is what God does with me all the time. He's so much stronger and faster, but He waits for me to follow. He waits for me to catch up to His way of going. It's slow, but I'm waddling forward.

Lord, lead me today in Your path. Show me the way and give me the stamina to keep moving forward in faith.

Good Gifts

Which of you, if your son asks for bread, will give him a stone? . . .
If you, then, though you are evil, know how to give good gifts
to your children, how much more will your Father in
heaven give good gifts to those who ask him!

MATTHEW 7:9–11 NIV

Some things spring into my memory: the jingle of my childhood dog's license tags; the gentle muscle of Mom's hand; the squeal of oars in the aluminum rowboat's locks.

Our little Sheltie, Sandy, died when I was sixteen. She was fourteen. It's no wonder we were so attached. I loved that dog with, perhaps, my first unselfish love. I've rarely run into anyone who disagrees with that assessment, when we begin speaking about our childhood pets. I think the memory of that dog was one major reason that I eventually accepted the idea of a loving God. God's gifts are many and varied; each one is a door for testifying about a God who is good enough to send us such gifts, a God who loves us enough to send us a Savior.

God of all goodness, help me to see the gifts You send;
help me to see You in those gifts; and help me to share You—
as the Giver of great gifts—with those I know.

Comfort for the Weary

Come to me, all you who are weary and burdened,
and I will give you rest.
MATTHEW 11:28 NIV

"Sassy, how about a camping trip?" Janene asked her canine companion. Although the elderly Sassy was nearly blind and deaf, the dog came to life and jumped up and down with her whole-body answer, "Yes!"

Janene set up camp away from the road. At first it seemed like just another overnighter. Janene and Sassy were both having a great time. But in the early hours of the morning, Janene was awakened by the sound of barking, yipping, and creatures sprinting through the dry brush near her tent. She knew wolves had recently been rereleased in the wooded area where they were camping. She also knew that wolves are vicious predators. *The wolves can probably smell Sassy,* Janene thought. *If they find her, she's breakfast. She's so helpless!*

Janene pulled Sassy close. She knew the tent was not enough protection. She unzipped it while carrying the dog and sleeping bag to the truck. Though the night, Sassy snoozed peacefully on Janene's chest inside the wolf-proof vehicle.

Just as Janene took Sassy to a safe place and stayed with her, God stands guard over us when we are weary and unable to handle things on our own. Exhaustion often comes from too many demands on our time and energy. That's when God gives us comfort and a safe place.

Lord, thank You for extra comfort,
protection, and strength whenever I need it.

Baby Steps

For we walk by faith, not by sight.
2 CORINTHIANS 5:7 KJV

Born two months premature, I wasn't expected to develop physically at the pace of a full-term baby. The pediatrician told my mother he didn't expect me to walk before I reached fifteen months.

As soon as I had mastered the art of crawling, our collie, Toni, stretched out next to me on the floor. I wrapped my tiny fingers around hunks of her fur. Toni slowly stood, and to my mother's amazement, pulled me up with her. She took a step, then looked back at me, waiting for me to move forward. Another step followed, and another, until I lost my grip and plopped back to the floor. Toni lay down again and gave me another try.

My mother encouraged us, praising both collie and child, while at the same time paying close attention to Toni's demeanor. Would the dog snap at me if I pulled too hard? Not this patient trainer.

I learned to pull myself up by grabbing her fur while she stood. Toni offered her daily lesson until we walked steadily together from the living room to the kitchen and into my mother's waiting arms.

The doctor happily ate his words when he saw me walking on my own at twelve months.

Precious Jesus, thank You for Your patience with us, Your servants, as we take baby steps in our faith and grow in our understanding of Your Word.

163

Having a Ball

The precepts of the LORD are right, giving joy to the heart.
PSALM 19:8 NIV

Friskie the terrier joined our family three weeks ago. She greets me each morning with a wagging tail and a rubber ball in her mouth. I throw the ball and she retrieves it. There's only one problem. She won't give the ball back. Friskie fetches and flops down on her belly a yard away with the ball clenched in her jaws. She clearly wants to continue the game, but on her own terms. I reach for the toy and she bows, tail wagging, and skips farther away. I am not as fond of chase as she is, so the game ends unless she will surrender her prize. Eventually she realizes things have come to a halt and brings me the ball. Then the cycle starts over again.

As funny as I find Friskie's lack of awareness, I must admit that I am often guilty of the same error. I ask the Lord to help me with a problem, then continue to worry about it and create mental scenarios (usually worst-case scenarios) that keep me awake all night. I pray, surrendering my children to His care, and then fret over every decision they make. The truth is, I love to feel as if I'm in control. In reality I am only fighting against what would bring me the greatest joy—complete reliance on my wonderful, all-knowing Savior.

Dear Lord, I choose to enjoy Your friendship and Lordship today.

Symba's Last Run

Let us not love with words or speech
but with actions and in truth.
1 JOHN 3:18 NIV

One day while my wife was out, I took our very old collie, Symba, for his afternoon walk. He was having great difficulty walking. Just stepping up the five-inch curbs was a struggle. We were across the street and several houses down when my wife drove home. Symba heard the car and started tugging at the leash with more strength than I thought he had. There were no other cars moving on the street, so after my wife pulled into the driveway, I nervously let Symba off the leash. He ran; he was stiff with arthritis, but he ran. He leaped—yes, leaped—down the curb, across the street, then up the curb to my wife. I thought he was going to break a bone. He was about the happiest creature I'd ever seen.

It hurt him to do it. I almost had to lift him up the three steps to the front door.

Here's one lesson I take from this: When we've known the selfless love of a good dog, how can we not instantly recognize and despise selfishness, especially in ourselves?

How can we not feel the unutterable emptiness of selfishness?

You, Lord, gave of Your love until it hurt. You ran to us, though it killed You. Help me to love those around me until it hurts. . .and then love them some more.

The Resting Place

Whoever dwells in the shelter of the Most High
will rest in the shadow of the Almighty.

PSALM 91:1 NIV

For three years, the dogs' sleeping crate was in the northwest corner of the living room. During redecoration, we moved it to the southwest corner to make room for a bookcase. When we ordered the dogs to bed that night, Jot headed straight for the crate and started pawing the blankets for a comfortable nest. Tilly walked to the bookcase and stood facing it, clearly confused. We had a good laugh, picked her up, and put her in the newly relocated crate. Three months later, she was still having a frustrating face-off with the bookcase at least one night a week. Tilly has brain damage as a result of abuse at a young age, and it affects her long-term memory. Eventually she learned the new location of the crate and happily lies down with Jot at night in her nice, secure place.

King David knew the value of a good resting place. In Psalm 91, David refers to God as "shelter," "refuge," "fortress," "shield," "rampart," "dwelling," and "tent." He praises God's ability to keep him secure by being his "cover," "guard," "rescue," and "savior."

Are you seeking refuge in the wrong place? Or do you seek the face of your Refuge?

Dear Lord, my refuge, I choose today to dwell in Your presence. Be my cover, guide, and Savior as I rest in You.

When the Doorbell Rings

I give them eternal life, and they shall never perish;
no one will snatch them out of my hand. My Father,
who has given them to me, is greater than all;
no one can snatch them out of my Father's hand.

JOHN 10:28–29 NIV

Roko considered it his primary duty to answer the door, even though the happy dance of a ninety-pound retriever could flatten a quarterback in full uniform and pads.

When the doorbell rang, Carlie struggled with the dog while she tried to open the door, but Roko was still prancing around, barking. Finally, she grabbed him by the collar and ordered him to sit down. His wiggling body responded slowly.

Carlie's guest gasped. "I thought all your retrievers went to obedience school. What happened? Did this one flunk out?"

"Nope. He passed. He gets excited, but he'll settle down. Roko! Lie down!" Carlie pointed to a comfortable spot. Roko lay down and soon was snoring. All was quiet for now—until the next time the doorbell rang.

Have you dwelled upon past moments and choices that disappoint God? He still loves you. Red-faced memories? He still loves you. Mistakes? He still loves you.

But more than that, He forgives and forgets our misdeeds. We still have the promise of life with Him forever. And while on earth, He's a great mentor, as well.

Lord, thanks for Your gift of forgiveness and eternal life.
I can let my red-faced moments go.

Forgiveness

Be kind and compassionate to one another,
forgiving each other, just as in Christ God forgave you.
EPHESIANS 4:32 NIV

I ran in to get my mom's help with the dog bite on my leg. It was bleeding. I faked a little panic.

"Which dog bit you?"

I waited with a dramatic pause. "Sandy." (Our beloved Sheltie.)

Mom's eyes popped open wide. She couldn't believe it. So I told her the story.

"Sandy was running beside me as I rode my bike. She stumbled and fell right in front of me, and I accidentally rode over her snout. She yelped and jumped up and bit me."

Although she was injured, that great little dog never held it against me that I ran over her nose. She didn't even shy away from the bike. How could I ever be angry at her? She just reacted with instinct. After she bit me, she acted ashamed of herself and tried to comfort me.

Forgiveness. It's a beautiful thing.

Savior, help us to forgive others as You have forgiven us.
Especially help us to give the hardest forgiveness
of all to those closest to us.

Furry Comforter

And I will ask the Father, and he will give you another
advocate to help you and be with you forever—the Spirit of truth.
JOHN 14:16–17 NIV

Yesterday I attended an event at our library called Children Reading
to Dogs. Children and their parents rotated on the carpeted library
floor to four different dogs and handlers.

The librarian explained, "Children who are intimidated by
reading aloud to people will read fearlessly to dogs." I observed
parents' peaceful faces as their children read. Dogs sniffed hands
and illustrated books being read—mutual interest exchanged
between the reader and listener.

"Under the 'Lend a Heart Program,' we also take dogs to
the airport," the librarian added. "Yesterday, I had my Australian
shepherd at the waiting area. People come by to stroke her and have
conversation. It calms their nerves before a flight. One man stopped
last week and sat down to talk. When he got up, he smiled and told
me that he had been on the way to the bar for a glass of wine to help
him relax, but that he didn't feel like he needed to go now."

Animals can provide temporary comfort and needed attention.
Pets can bring us the loving presence we thrive in.

Jesus said when He left, He would send His followers the Holy
Spirit, who would be with us forever—our loving Comforter and
Counselor who would never leave us.

**Thank You, Lord, for sending Your Holy Spirit to comfort
and counsel me. Remind me of Your presence as You walk
with me through today's challenges or trials.**

Good Gifts

"Every good and perfect gift is from above,
coming down from the Father of the heavenly lights,
who does not change like shifting shadows."
JAMES 1:17 NIV

Ginger loves to leave gifts on our doorstep. Then she sits there, excitedly wagging her tail while she waits for us to find whatever it is. The "better" the gift, the more excited she gets.

In the last month, she's brought us a dead frog, an old rotting newspaper, and various scraps of things she's dug up from around the yard. This morning, she brought an enormous catfish head, which she must have found in the pond. That's some kind of gift.

While Ginger's gifts are sometimes questionable, God's gifts to us are always good. He knows what we like and don't like, and He knows the desires of our hearts. He also knows what will benefit us for eternity, as opposed to what will only make us happy for a little while.

Sometimes, when we don't get what we want, it seems like God has left us off His divine gift list—but nothing could be further from the truth. God adores us, and He is excited to give us things that will make us smile, make us happy, and make us more like Him.

Dear Father, thank You for Your good gifts to me. Help me to recognize and appreciate those gifts when they come. Most of all, thank You for Jesus and for what He did for me on the cross.

The Telltale Path

Stand at the crossroads and look; ask for the ancient paths,
ask where the good way is, and walk in it,
and you will find rest for your souls.

JEREMIAH 6:16 NIV

Kathy came home to find a bag of potatoes ripped open on the kitchen floor. She went looking for her dogs, Myrna and Tillie. Tillie was nowhere to be found, but Myrna stood ready to lead Kathy to the guilty party.

As Kathy followed Myrna into the living room, she discovered a potato trail. None had been eaten, but every one of them (and there were many) had one set of teeth marks. The trail markers led to the bedroom. Tillie the potato thief sat on the carpet looking as guilty as a basset hound can look.

Even before Jeremiah's day, God told His people there are paths for them to follow. The psalmist said, "Show me your ways, LORD, teach me your paths" (Psalm 25:4 NIV). In Isaiah a promise reads, "The LORD will guide you always" (Isaiah 58:11 NIV). When Thomas told Jesus he didn't know where He was going, Jesus replied, "I am the way and the truth and the life" (John 14:6 NIV). God doesn't leave tooth-marked potatoes or bread crumbs to show us the way we should go. He provided His very Son as the way to heaven. Jesus is the good—and only—way to the Father.

Lord, thank You for the Bible,
which clearly shows me how to reach You.

Step Out of Your Comfort Zone

"My grace is all you need. My power works best in weakness."
So now I am glad to boast about my weaknesses,
so that the power of Christ can work through me.

2 CORINTHIANS 12:9 NLT

My husband, Blaine, received a promotion, and it meant a move to the Midwest. Several delays in closings on our old house forced us to live in a hotel for three weeks. I was concerned about how this would affect Romeo. He wasn't very social and normally barked at dogs and people, because he didn't perceive himself to be a dog in the first place.

Within just a few days, he stepped out of his comfort zone and became the official hall greeter. He is a small, fluffy half shih tzu, half dachshund, so people always notice him. His unexpected new personality surprised me, and even forced me to talk to anyone and everyone.

Up and down the halls of the hotel, in the lobby and outside for our walks, Romeo took on this friendly persona. He was enthusiastic about greeting everyone, from the elite to the homeless. He was no respecter of persons; he checked everyone out. So often we can be quick to judge others based on their appearances, but Romeo decided we should give everyone an opportunity to know us.

Father, sometimes I can be judgmental or stereotype people based on their appearance. Help me to step out of my comfort zone and speak Your love to everyone.

Snoring Zoey

Love suffers long and is kind; love does not envy;
love does not parade itself, is not puffed up; does not behave
rudely, does not seek its own, is not provoked, thinks no evil;
does not rejoice in iniquity, but rejoices in the truth; bears all
things, believes all things, hopes all things, endures all things.
1 CORINTHIANS 13:4–7 NKJV

I woke to the sound of snoring, so I nudged my husband to make
him roll over. As soon as I did, he jolted awake, and I realized it was
not him snoring. It was our dog, Zoey. I apologized to my husband—
but what was I supposed to do with a snoring dog? I've tossed a
pillow at her, which worked pretty well for about three seconds. I've
called her name, which is much more effective. This lasted about
four seconds. She is loud, but if you lock her out of the room she
whines on the other side of the door.

I've learned to sleep through it, something that may be helping
my husband, as well, now that I think about it.

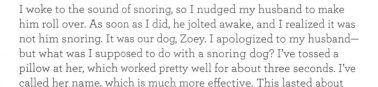

Lord, give me the grace to work through the inconveniences
that come my way today. I need Your indwelling
love to accomplish that.

Heaven and Earth

Thy will be done in earth, as it is in heaven.
MATTHEW 6:10 KJV

I think that Symba, my collie, has a heaven. I think he goes there several times a day.

I have a semi-deflated soccer ball that I kick to him in the backyard. Sometimes he brings it back to me. Sometimes he plays keep-away, letting me lunge within an inch of grabbing it before he yanks it away, circles, and does it again.

I can tell when he's dreaming about his little keep-away game, by the way he moves his legs, head, and mouth—and by the way he wags his tail.

Symba has a heaven. He goes there in his dreams. It makes him more eager to live out his dreams in the real world. Sometimes I even wonder, by the look he gives me when he wakes up, which world is more real to him.

We have a heaven. How often do we go there, in prayer, in our own dreams, or in our thoughts? How real is it to us? And how hard do we work to bring that heaven—as Jesus called it, "the kingdom of heaven"—to our little piece of the earth?

Jesus, please make Your heaven real to me; not so I can avoid responsibilities, but so I can saturate them with the joy that is there, and draw people to the One who lives there.

About Temptation

Watch and pray so that you will not fall into temptation.
The spirit is willing, but the flesh is weak.
MARK 14:38 NIV

Tilly the rat terrier stands nine inches tall at the shoulder. She can propel herself onto the kitchen counter with a mighty spring of her four-inch legs. I have occasionally found Tilly in the sink, casually licking the dinner plates. My husband calls it the "pre-wash cycle." I have given up scolding Tilly when I find her enjoying this forbidden treat, since she never looks in the least repentant. Nor should she! Tilly is doing what dogs are supposed to do—taking advantage of food when it is available. She does not know temptation, but understands opportunity when she sees (or smells) it. She doesn't understand that there will always be another meal provided at the right time.

I, on the other hand, am very aware of both God's constant provision and His just laws. I can trust Him to give me what I need and withhold that which would harm me. Why, then, do I desire unwholesome things? My flesh craves self-governance. I want to be in control. The best antidote for this sort of selfishness is spending time with God every day. Prayer and listening for His voice remind me of His goodness and righteousness. When I am in His presence, I don't need to be in control.

Jehovah Jireh, my Provider, give me peace today to trust You.
I place myself under Your compassionate and loving control.

Scents of Joy

*Now thanks be to God who always leads us in triumph
in Christ, and through us diffuses the fragrance
of His knowledge in every place.*

2 CORINTHIANS 2:14 NKJV

We dog-sat Bobby, a fifteen-year-old miniature poodle, while a friend moved out of state. During the first week, I took him for a checkup.

Our veterinarian reported Bobby was in good health, except for missing his canine teeth. She explained it wasn't unusual for dogs of his age to lose them. But left untreated, food particles and other debris had gathered in the empty cavities, which connected to his nostrils. She anesthetized Bobby, cleaned out each opening, then sutured them closed.

The next day, I walked a woozy Bobby out of the clinic on his leash. He stopped, perked up his ears, and raised his nose in the air. His powder-puff tail wagged like a cheerleader's pom-pom.

At home, he sprinted from the car to the oak tree, then to the bushes, sniffing each of them. Then he dashed to the flowers and gleefully inhaled a lungful of their sweet fragrance.

He ran into the house and sniffed the plants, the furniture, even the cats—much to their chagrin. Anything his little black nose could reach added to his excitement. We couldn't help but share in his delight at the renewed sense of smell.

**Gracious Lord, Bobby gave us an insight into the joy
we can experience in the sweet fragrance
of Your presence in every place.**

Healing Comes

A time to heal. . .a time to mend.
ECCLESIASTES 3:3, 7 NIV

When my yellow Lab, Sammy, was a puppy, a friend of mine asked me to bring him to her house. A big dog had attacked her husband while he was holding their firstborn, Jordan. Now her husband and their four children were all terrified of dogs.

"Sammy likes to chase tennis balls and chew on bones," I told them the first time we visited. My friend's husband and the boys watched us from several yards away. I threw a ball, and little Sammy chased it, pushing it with his pink nose and bracing it with his mouth and paws. The boys giggled. "Can I throw the ball?" asked Golan, who was five. He grinned as Sammy chased the ball. Six-year-old Jordan stepped forward and reached for the leash. "Can I walk him?" He proudly paraded the twenty-plus-pound puppy around the backyard patio.

Six months later, we visited again. Sixty-pound Sammy wagged his tail as we entered the yard. My friend's husband tentatively watched his sons run to greet Sam and stroke him. Golan handed me a crayon drawing of a yellow smiling dog with a green ball. A year later, we stepped through the door to cheers of joy. "Sammy's here!" the boys yelled. Their father walked over to pet my 120-pound Lab. "Hi, Sammy," he said.

Today the family has a dog of their own.

Thank You, Lord, for healing times.

Knowing God

Come near to God and he will come near to you.
JAMES 4:8 NIV

My friends asked me to feed their dogs while they were away. They had a mama and papa dog and new puppies. Papa dog was always happy to see me. Mama dog, on the other hand, treated me like I was some kind of lowlife bottom-dweller, there to steal her babies.

Each day, I let myself into their house. Papa would bark and jump and wag his tail, and I could barely get in the door because of his excitement. But Mama was nowhere to be seen. I had to go looking for her.

She was usually in the back room with her puppies. The minute I came near, she bared her teeth and growled. I saved my cuddles for Papa, and simply left Mama's bowls full of food and water.

She didn't know I was a safe person because she wasn't familiar with me. If only she realized I was there to help her, not harm her. If only she understood I wanted to take care of her and make her life better.

Sometimes I feel afraid of what God has in store for me. I worry that He'll lead me into all sorts of gloom and doom. That's when I have to check myself. How well do I know my Father? How much time have I spent with Him lately? God is a loving, kind, compassionate God, and He only wants good things for me. The more time I spend with Him, the more I understand that.

Dear Father, stay near me today. I want to know You more.

Fast Learner

They refused to pay attention. . . . They made their
hearts as hard as flint and would not listen.
ZECHARIAH 7:11–12 NIV

Izzy was a fast learner who only had to receive the weakest zap from
her training collar to learn her boundaries. Most dogs take at least
three days to make the association. Not Izzy. One small zap and she
stayed put. Shirley never had to inch the zapper up a notch to keep
Izzy inside the invisible fence.

Then there's Dixie. Because of Dixie's persistent barking,
her owners got her a collar to stop the unrelenting barking.
Unfortunately for Dixie and everyone else who must endure her
ceaseless yapping, the collar never worked, no matter what the
setting. Her family gave up. Dixie continues "barking up the wrong
tree" when it comes to winning new friends, or alerting her family to
any genuine danger.

When the Lord is trying to teach me a lesson, I wonder: Am I
like Izzy or Dixie? Do I learn with one gentle reminder or rebuke?
Or does the Lord have to repeatedly increase His divine "zap" to
get my attention or obedience? Am I like the people of the prophet
Zechariah's day to whom God finally said, "When I called, they did
not listen; so when they called, I would not listen" (Zechariah 7:13
NIV)? I hope not! I want to obey the first time, every time.

Lord, give me ears to hear and an eager willingness to obey.

The Power of Touch

He took the blind man by the hand and led him outside the village.
When he had spit on the man's eyes and put his hands on him,
Jesus asked, "Do you see anything?" He looked up and said,
"I see people; they look like trees walking around."

MARK 8:23–24 NIV

As empty nesters, Romeo, our half shih tzu, half dachshund, is our baby. We adopted him as a puppy when our youngest son was a freshman in high school. Romeo responds powerfully to the power of touch—actually, these days, he demands it.

If there's no room on the couch for him to jump up, he'll pout pitifully until one of us picks him up and puts him in our lap. If he's feeling a little neglected, he'll whine until one of us gets down on the floor with him so he can touch us. He'll lay his head on my leg or roll over so that his back is touching part of my body. Touch makes you feel good and Romeo knows it. Wherever we are, he wants to be connected to us.

It's easy for me to focus on the task at hand and forget to greet coworkers or take time to develop relationships with others. Romeo reminds me that we need to connect with others and show affection to people we love.

Father, help me to show love and affection through
the power of touch—especially with my spouse and family.
Give me opportunities to demonstrate how
important they are to me.

Zoey in the Driver's Seat

Create in me a clean heart, O God, and renew a steadfast spirit within me. Do not cast me away from Your presence, and do not take Your Holy Spirit from me. Restore to me the joy of Your salvation and uphold me by Your generous Spirit.
PSALM 51:10–13 NKJV

A friend was going with me to Oak Openings to hike and hammock together. She arrived at my house and we loaded into my car. When I ran into the house to get my water bottle, I left the driver's side door open. I returned my to find my dog, Zoey, sitting in the driver's seat, ready to go. My friend looked at me with uncertainty, "I didn't know what to do, so we're just sitting here." So funny!

Zoey just didn't want to miss an opportunity for adventure. She didn't get to go on this one, but hey, it was worth a try. I love that she is eager to jump in and go. She's so willing to be my companion, even if she has no idea what she is getting herself into. Funny that my friend was in the same category that day. She had never been hammocking in the woods, but she went along and hung out in the trees in our camp hammocks. It was refreshing to walk and relax in the beauty of God's creation that day.

Lord, foster a spirit of adventure in me that I may discover what You have for me today, even in the simplest of things.

Sandy's Discernment

*To every thing there is a season,
and a time to every purpose under the heaven.*
ECCLESIASTES 3:1 KJV

The German shepherd cocked her head. Her sweet expression melted my heart like Kryptonite. I told the man holding the leash that he had found a home for the stray. Her tan-colored coat reminded me of the beach, so I named her Sandy.

After a checkup with my vet, I drove her home to meet my cat. To my surprise, they bonded immediately.

We took a walk that evening. When a jogger approached a little too close, Sandy snarled, tugged at the leash, and barked her warning. He crossed the street and continued his run on the other side. Sandy held her ferocious stance, watching him—teeth still bared—until he disappeared around the corner. She relaxed and gave me the green light to resume our walk.

The next day, I allowed her a supervised front yard adventure. Neighborhood children flocked to her. She lolled in the grass and allowed them to pet her, crawl over her, and pull on her ears. One little boy stuck his arm inside her mouth. I almost panicked, but Sandy didn't chomp down. She kept her mouth open and flipped his arm with her tongue. The child giggled with delight.

Sandy looked at me with grateful eyes and pounded the lawn with her wagging tail.

Father God, through Sandy's discernment, You taught me there is a time to be assertive and a time for gentleness.

A Blessing in Disguise

And we know that in all things God works for the good of those
who love him, who have been called according to his purpose.
ROMANS 8:28 NIV

When Robyn and Alan were newlyweds, they purchased their first
dog, a Dalmatian puppy named Mila.

Days after they brought her home, they stood over her bed,
calling her name. She slept like a baby until they touched her—
Robyn was devastated. "Mila will be fine. She'll adjust," said the vet
assistant, who also owned a deaf Dalmatian. She reassured Robyn
with her dog stories.

When Robyn and Alan notified the breeder, he apologized,
offering to send them another. He would put Mila down. Horrified,
they refused to send her back, and he gave them another Dalmatian
puppy. Sophie joined their home.

Sophie barked at Mila when they were introduced. Mila
didn't respond. Sophie nudged her with her nose and Mila pushed
Sophie with her paw. Sophie never barked at Mila again—she
communicated by touch. They played well together and loved each
other. On river walks, if Mila headed the wrong direction, Sophie
herded her back.

Robyn considers those years as God's way of preparing her and
Alan for parenting two children.

Many times we have expectations about experiences in life that
can twist to disappointment. But if we take each day and just do the
next step, trusting God to help us, He can turn disaster to delight.

Thank You, God, for abounding grace
at difficult times. Help me to listen
and lean upon You for direction and peace.

Starving Hearts

A pack of dogs lives near our home. They roam the streets, finding food where they can and threatening anyone who comes near. Their ribs show in skeletal misery.

We recently found them outside our chicken pen, looking hungrily at the birds inside. We ran them off, but we worry they'll be back. It's a sad situation; one I'm not sure will end well. The dogs are doing what they must to survive. If they had someone to love and care for them, they wouldn't be looking to cause harm to innocent prey.

Many people in this world walk around with starved, skeletal spirits. They're sad and lonely, hungry for love and affection. They hurt people because they've been hurt. Instead of viewing these people with disdain, we need to see them as God does: as people who need kindness and compassion. If we'll gently offer them the love they need, their skeletal frames will eventually plump up, and they'll have the opportunity to transform into a gentle reflection of His grace.

**Dear Father, help me to see others the way You see them.
Help me to feed hungry bodies with food
and hungry spirits with Your love.**

That Sixth Sense

*Surely the Sovereign L*ord *does nothing without revealing his plan to his servants the prophets.*
Amos 3:7 niv

Assistance dogs give support, companionship, and practical help to children and adults who have debilitating limitations or conditions. These dogs are trained well at no small expense, but their worth is immeasurable. Even without intensive training, some dogs have a sixth sense that comes only from God.

Arina had not been sick and had not made any changes in her daily routine. Yet Willy followed her around the house like the proverbial lost puppy. The little poodle refused to let his teenage mistress out of his sight. Inside or out, upstairs or down, whenever Arina turned around, Willy was right underfoot. After a steady week of this, Arina finally confronted her poodle.

"What do you *want*?" She turned to her mother. "What is his problem?"

Turns out it wasn't Willy who had the problem. After years of being seizure-free despite her epilepsy, that Friday at school Arina had a major seizure. She hadn't known it was coming, nor had her parents. But somehow Willy knew—and afterward he stopped dogging Arina's every step.

The Lord knows all, including the future. Sometimes His "nudges" come from people like the Old Testament prophets; sometimes through our pets. Sometimes through a "gentle whisper" (1 Kings 19:12 niv). Do we have ears to hear and heed Him?

**Dear Father, give me ears to hear
what You have to say to me today.**

Sleeping Siren

Search me, O God, and know my heart; try me and know my anxieties; and see if there is any wicked way in me, and lead me in the way everlasting.

PSALM 139:23–24 NKJV

Before Zoey's son, Frank, moved away to California with my son, Frank's master, the two dogs would howl together whenever they heard sirens. Frank was always the louder of the two. Zoey has taken some time to adjust to being the lone dog at the house, and sometimes I wonder if she still thinks of Frank. I've noticed that she doesn't howl at sirens consistently anymore, like she did when Frank was home.

One afternoon as I sat working on my laptop, Zoey lay napping on the floor when a siren went off in the streets nearby. She suddenly began to howl in her sleep and woke herself up with her own noise. I couldn't help but wonder if she had been dreaming of Frank. I wonder if she was processing life in the depths of sleep the way that humans do, so we hopefully awake a little more whole than the night before.

God, thank You for the restoration of sleep and dreaming. Today, show me in my waking moments what You want me to see, so that my heart may move toward healing in the broken places.

Contributors

Dee Aspin, a freelance writer, worked as a hospital RN, and volunteered with Juvenile Justice Chaplaincy and Christian Singles' groups for three decades in her native California. She authored a book called *Lord of the Ringless* and is now married. Dee has written for CBN, Guideposts, Revel, and more. Visit Dee at *www.DeeAspin.com* Her readings can be found on pages 7, 18, 26, 35, 46, 54, 63, 72, 81, 91, 100, 109, 119, 127, 138, 146, 156, 169, 177, and 183.

Renae Brumbaugh lives in Texas with two noisy children and two dogs. She has authored four books in Barbour's Camp Club Girls series. Her readings can be found on pages 8, 19, 27, 36, 47, 55, 64, 73, 82, 92, 101, 110, 120, 128, 139, 147, 157, 170, 178, and 184.

Katherine Douglas has authored numerous articles and books, and contributed to several anthologies. She enjoys leading women's Bible studies at her church. Katherine and her husband live in Fulton County, Ohio. Her readings can be found on pages 9, 20, 28, 37, 48, 56, 65, 74, 83, 93, 102, 111, 121, 129, 140, 148, 158, 171, 179, and 185.

Shanna D. Gregor is a freelance writer, editor, and product developer who has served various ministries and publishers. The mother of two young men, Shanna and her husband reside in Tucson, Arizona. Her readings can be found on pages 10, 21, 29, 38, 49, 57, 66, 75, 84, 94, 103, 112, 122, 130, 141, 149, 159, 172, and 180.

Glenn A. Hascall is an accomplished writer with credits in more than fifty books. His articles have appeared in numerous publications, including the *Wall Street Journal*. His readings can be found on pages 12, 31, 45, 62, 80, 90, 105, 124, 132, and 151.

Ardythe Kolb writes articles and devotions for various publications and is currently working on her third book. She serves on the advisory board of a writers' network and edits their newsletter. Her readings can be found on pages 13, 23, 32, 40, 51, 59, 68, 86, 114, and 133.

Shelley R. Lee is the author of *Before I Knew You*, *Mat Madness*, and numerous magazine and newspaper articles. She has contributed to several Barbour projects, including the *Daily Wisdom for Women 2014 Devotional Collection*. She resides in northwest Ohio with her husband of twenty nine years, David, and their four grown sons. Her readings can be found on pages 11, 22, 30, 39, 50, 58, 67, 76, 85, 95, 104, 113, 123, 131, 142, 150, 160, 173, 181, and 186.

Emily Marsh lives in Virginia with her husband, Seth, and their various pit bull foster puppies. She works at a downtown real estate firm as a client care coordinator and talso teaches ballet in her spare time. Her readings can be found on pages 14, 24, 33, 41, 52, 60, 69, 77, 87, and 96.

Chuck Miller lives in Sylvania Township, Ohio. He worked for fourteen years as a high school English, journalism and Bible teacher, in the public schools of Lexington, Kentucky, and then at Toledo Christian Schools. He worked as a hospital chaplain—nights and weekends, the "disaster shift"—for seven years; and currently works in the surgical instrument department of that hospital and as a freelance writer of devotions and poetry. Some of his devotional work and poetry can be found on his website, BardofChrist.net. He's been married for forty-two years; his four-year-old grandson, Preston (aka "Pres-Tron"!), is the joy of his life. His readings can be found on pages 97, 106, 115, 125, 134, 143, 152, 161, 165, 168, and 174.

Widely published author **Connie L. Peters** writes adult and children's fiction, creative and inspirational nonfiction, and poetry from Cortez, Colorado, where she and her husband host two adults with developmental disabilities. Her readings can be found on pages 15, 25, 42, 70, 78, 98, 116, 135, 144, and 153.

Janet Ramsdell Rockey is a freelance Christian writer living in Tampa, Florida, with her Realtor husband and their two cats. She has written other works for Barbour Publishing, including the 180-day devotional, *Discovering God in Everyday Moments*. Her readings can be found on pages 145, 155, 163, 176, and 182.

Jo Russell is a Christian speaker, blogger, and longtime author of articles and anthology contributions, including several *Chicken Soup for the Soul* anthologies and the award-winning *Which Button Do You Push to Get God to Come Out? A Humorous Devotional for Women*. Her website, www.button-to-god.com, features a weekly humorous blog. She lives in northeast Arizona with her husband, Ed. Her readings can be found on pages 16, 43, 79, 88, 107, 117, 136, 154, 162, and 167.

Paula Swan is an artist and teacher from Toledo, Ohio, where she lives with her husband of eighteen years and their five pets. Her first publication was at the age of six. Paula attributes her love of words to the influence of her grandfather, Chester Arthur Smith, who taught her to read. She shares his passion for fairy tales and legends. She is an active member of Holland Free Methodist Church. Her readings can be found on pages 17, 71, 164, 166, and 175.

Cheryl Elaine Williams, resident of Pittsburgh, Pennsylvania, is involved with family and church activities, gardening, and crafting for craft shows. She recently took two rescue animals into her house. She's published in Sweet Teen Young Adult fiction and in *Chicken Soup*–type anthologies, including Barbour Books' *Heavenly Humor for the Cat Lover's Soul*. Her readings can be found on pages 34, 44, 53, 61, 89, 99, 108, 118, 126, and 137.

Scripture Index